12.50
NN

A SCIENTIFIC THEORY
OF CULTURE

A SCIENTIFIC THEORY

OF CULTURE AND OTHER ESSAYS

By BRONISLAW MALINOWSKI

With a Preface by HUNTINGTON CAIRNS

THE UNIVERSITY OF NORTH CAROLINA PRESS
CHAPEL HILL

© 1944 by The University of North Carolina Press
All rights reserved
Manufactured in the United States of America
ISBN 0-8078-0433-9
Library of Congress Catalog Card Number 44-8385
First printing, September 1944
Second printing, November 1945
Third printing, January 1949
Fourth printing, May 1956
Fifth printing, May 1965
Sixth printing, September 1973
Seventh printing, February 1976
Eighth printing, December 1977
Ninth printing, November 1979

PREFACE

THIS VOLUME is both a summing up and a reformulation of Professor Bronislaw Malinowski's functional theory of culture. Some of its ideas in embryonic form may be found on the first page of his first book, published more than thirty years ago; others, at least in their developments, are new. Altogether the work presents the mature views in a field of great importance of one of the most brilliant and influential anthropologists who has appeared in the history of that subject. Those views, as they are here set forth, are the product of fierce controversy. Their lot has thus been the happiest that can befall ideas: they have been subjected to the minute scrutiny of experts attached to rival positions. That they have withstood, except for minor modifications, the analysis they have undergone is evidence of their vitality.

Bronislaw Malinowski was born in Cracow, Poland, on April 7, 1884. His first training was in mathematics and the physical sciences; the results of this discipline are clearly apparent in his sure grasp of the basic elements of scientific method. At the same time he remained free from the dogmatism usually associated with the study of the exact sciences. His interests were diverted to cultural anthropology by Wilhelm Wundt. Although his basic field-work was done in New Guinea and Northwestern Melanesia, particularly in the Trobriand Islands, he also spent briefer intervals with some Australian tribes, the Hopi of Arizona, the Bemba and Chagga of East Africa and the Zapotec of Mexico. Early encouragement came to him from scholars of a distinctly encyclopaedic approach—Wundt, Westermarck, Hobhouse, Frazer, Ellis—but his own practice was in the strictest accord with the contemporary standards which require a meticulous knowledge of the

whole life of individual tribes. His absorption of the culture of the Trobrianders was probably as complete as is
possible for any field investigation, and was conducted with
full benefit of modern methods, which include a knowledge
of the language and controls in the form of actual illustra-
tions for all general statements obtained from the natives.
From that preoccupation with the life of the Trobrianders
emerged the great series of volumes in which their life is
depicted in all its complexity. As he pointed out, he, like
every empirical worker in any branch of science, had to see
what appeared to him the general and universal in the
range of facts which he observed. But he always urged that
the final decision as to the validity, throughout the whole
range of sociological phenomena, of his general views,
based as they were on his specific knowledge of the Trobrianders, could only be determined after those conclusions had been tested in all the enthnographic areas still
open to observation.

Side by side with the prosecution of his exceptionally
thorough field-work he had an unremitting concern with
the development of theory. He had something of Plato's
admiration for the beauty inherent in the perfection of an
ordered body of propositions. Theory satisfied that "independent hunger of the mind" which leads in the end to
knowledge. He also saw theory in its practical aspects, not
only as the instrument which enabled the field-worker to
anticipate his solutions, but, in the modern logical view, as
explanation. He never tired of insisting that the great need
in anthropology was for more theoretical analysis, particularly analysis born from actual contact with natives. In that
aspect theory was the instrument which allowed inquiry to
be something more than a mere fumbling with multitudi-
nous possibilities; it was an indispensable guide to the
field-worker in the selection of facts; it was a necessary element in any sound descriptive science. But culture as a
whole, no less than the particular tribal practice, stood in
need of explanation. He was convinced that cultural

phenomena were not the consequence of capricious inventiveness or simple borrowing, but were determined by basic needs and the possibilities of satisfying them. This functional concept, he held, accounted for variety and differentiation, as well as for the common measure in the variety. The present volume is his last sustained elaboration of that idea.

Professor Malinowski died on May 16, 1942. At the request of Mrs. Bronislaw Malinowska I undertook to see the manuscript through the press. Fortunately, Professor Malinowski himself had revised the typed manuscript as far as 200 and I was thus able to confine corrections to typographical and other obvious errors. Professor Malinowski's basic approach is clarified further by the inclusion in this volume of two hitherto unpublished essays. I am indebted to Mrs. Bronislaw Malinowska and Mr. Blake Eggen for their assistance in the preparation of the book for publication.

HUNTINGTON CAIRNS

Washington, D. C.
February 15, 1944

CONTENTS

CONTENTS

A SCIENTIFIC THEORY
OF CULTURE

I CULTURE AS THE SUBJECT OF SCIENTIFIC INVESTIGATION

THE "Study of Man" is certainly a somewhat presumptuous, not to say preposterous, label when applied to academic anthropology as it now stands. A variety of disciplines, old and recent, venerable and new, deal also with inquiries into human nature, human handiwork, and into the relations between human beings. These can claim, one and all, to be regarded as branches of the legitimate Study of Man. The oldest, of course, are the contributions to moral philosophy, to theology, to more-or-less legendary history, and to the interpretations of old law and custom. Such contributions can be traced back to cultures still perpetuating the Stone Age; they certainly have flourished in the old civilizations of China and India, of Western Asia and Egypt. Economics and jurisprudence, political science and aesthetics, linguistics, archaeology, and the comparative study of religions, constitute a more recent addition to humanism. Some two centuries ago psychology, the study of the mind, and later on, sociology, an inquiry into human relations, were added to the list of official academic studies.

Anthropology, as the science of man at large, as the most comprehensive discipline in humanism without portfolio, was the last to come. It had to peg out its claims as to scope, subject matter, and method as best it could. It absorbed what was left over, and even had to encroach on some older preserves. It consists now of such studies as prehistory, folklore, physical anthropology, and cultural anthropology. These come dangerously near other legitimate fields of social and natural sciences: psychology, history, archaeology, sociology and anatomy.

3

The new science was born under the star of enthusiastic evolutionism, of anthropometric methods, and of revelatory discoveries in prehistory. No wonder that its original interests centered round the reconstruction of human beginnings, the search for the "missing link," and inquiries into parallels between prehistoric finds and ethnographic data. Looking back at the achievements of the last century, we could at worst see in them little more than an assemblage of antiquarian odds and ends, embracing ethnographic erudition, the measuring and counting of skulls and bones, and a collection of sensational data about our semi-human ancestors. This estimate, however, would certainly miss the best contributions of such pioneering students in comparative human cultures as Herbert Spencer and Adolf Bastian, E. B. Tylor and L. H. Morgan, General Pitt-Rivers and Frederick Ratzel, W. G. Sumner and R. S. Steinmetz, É. Durkheim and A. G. Keller. All these thinkers, as well as some of their successors, have been gradually working towards a scientific theory of human behavior, towards a better understanding of human nature, human society, and human culture.

Thus, in writing about the scientific approach to the Study of Man, an anthropologist has a task which, though perhaps not easy, is of some importance. It is his duty to define in what relation to one another the various branches of anthropology really stand. He has to determine the place which anthropology ought to occupy in the wider fraternity of humanistic studies. He has also to reopen the old question, in what sense humanism can be scientific.

In this essay I shall attempt to show that the real meeting-ground of all branches of anthropology is the scientific study of culture. As soon as the physical anthropologist recognizes that "race is as race does," he will also admit that no measurements, classifications, or descriptions of physical type have any relevancy unless and until we can correlate physical type with the cultural creativeness of a race. The task of the prehistorian and archaeologist is to reconstruct the full living reality of a past culture from partial evidence confined to material remnants. The ethnologist, again, who uses the evidence of present-day primitive and more advanced cultures in order to reconstruct human history in terms of either evolution or diffusion, can base his arguments on sound scientific data only if he understands what culture really is. Finally, the ethnographic field-worker cannot observe unless he knows what is relevant and essential, and is thus able to discard adventitious and fortuitous happenings. Thus, the scientific quota in all anthropological work consists in the theory of culture, with reference to the method of observation in the field and to the meaning of culture as process and product.

In the second place, I think that if anthropology can contribute towards a more scientific outlook on its legitimate subject matter, that is, culture, it will render an indispensable service to other humanities. Culture, as the widest context of human behavior, is as important to the psychologist as to the social student, to the historian as to the linguist. I submit that the linguistics of the future, especially as regards the science of meaning, will become the study of language in the context of culture. Again, economics as an inquiry into wealth and welfare, as means of exchange and production, may find it useful in the future not to consider economic man completely detached from other pursuits and considerations, but to base its principles and arguments on the study of man as he really is, moving in the complex, many-dimensional medium of cultural interests. Indeed, most of the modern tendencies in economics, whether labelled "institutional," "psychological," or "historical," are supplementing the old, purely economic theories by placing economic man within the context of his multiple drives, interests and habits, that is, man as he is molded by his complex, partly rational, partly emotional cultural setting.

Jurisprudence, again, is gradually tending to regard law not as a self-contained universe of discourse, but as one of the several systems of social control in which concepts of purpose, value, moral constraint, and customary force have to be considered, besides the purely formal apparatus of code, court, and constabulary. Thus, not merely anthropology, but the Study of Man in general, comprising all the social sciences, all the new psychologically or sociologically oriented disciplines, may and must coöperate in the building of a common scientific basis, which perforce will have to be identical for all the diverse pursuits of humanism.

II A MINIMUM DEFINITION OF SCIENCE FOR THE HUMANIST

IT REMAINS NOW to define more specifically why and in what manner anthropology, of all social studies, can claim to be a direct contributor towards making the Study of Man more scientific. I would like to state first that the scientific approach is obviously not the only interest or inspiration in the domain of humanism. Moral or philosophical points of view; aesthetic, humanitarian, or theological zeal or inspiration; the desire to know what the past was because the past appeals to our sentiments in a manner which need not be vindicated but cannot be gainsaid—all these are legitimate motivations in all humanities. Science, however, as a tool at least, as a means to an end, is indispensable.

As I shall try to point out, a genuine scientific method has been inherent in all historic work, in all chronicling, in every argument used in jurisprudence, economics, and linguistics. There is no such thing as description completely devoid of theory. Whether you reconstruct historic scenes, carry out a field investigation in a savage tribe or a civilized community, analyze statistics, or make inferences from an archaeological monument or a prehistoric find— every statement and every argument has to be made in words, that is, in concepts. Each concept, in turn, is the result of a theory which declares that some facts are relevant and others adventitious, that some factors determine the course of events and others are merely accidental byplay; that things happen as they do because personalities, masses, and material agencies of the environment produced them. The hackneyed distinction between nomothetic and ideographic disciplines is a philosophical red herring which a simple consideration of what it means to observe, to reconstruct or to state an historic fact ought to have annihilated long ago. The cause of all the trouble consists in the fact that most principles, generalizations, and theories were implicit in the historian's reconstruction, and were intuitive rather than systematic in nature. The typical historian and many anthropologists spend most of their theoretical energy and epistemological leisure hours in refuting the concept of scientific law in cultural process, in erecting watertight compartments for humanism as against science, and in claiming that the historian or anthropologist can conjure up the past by some specific insight, some intuition or revelation, in short, that he can rely on the grace of God instead of on a methodical system of conscientious work.

However we may define the word *science* in some philosophical or epistemological system, it is clear that it begins with the use of previous observation for the prediction of the future. In this sense the spirit as well as the performance of science must have existed in the reasonable behavior of man, even as he was embarking on his career of creating, constructing, and developing culture. Take any primitive art or craft, one of those with which culture probably started, which is developed and remolded, and has ever since remained at its very foundations: the art of making fire, of constructing implements out of wood or stone, of building rudimentary shelters, or of using caves for living. What assumptions have we to make concerning man's reasonable behavior, the permanent incorporation of such reasonable behavior in tradition, and the fidelity of each generation to the traditional knowledge inherited from their ancestors?

One of the simplest and most fundamental primitive

crafts is that of fire-making. In this, over and above the manual ability of the craftsman, we find a definite scientific theory embodied in each performance, and in the tribal tradition thereof. Such a tradition had to define in a general, that is, abstract manner, the material and form of the two types of wood used. The tradition also had to define the principles of performance, the type of muscular movement, its speed, the capture of the spark, and the nourishment of the flame. The tradition was kept alive not in books nor yet in explicit physical theories. But it implied two pedagogical and theoretical elements. First and foremost, it was embodied in the manual skills of each generation, which, by example and precept, were handed over to the new growing members. Secondly, whether primitive symbolism was accomplished by verbal statement, by significant gesture, or by substantial performance, such as instructions where to find and how to store the materials and produce the forms, such symbolism must have been at work, even as I myself have seen it at work in my field research. That this is so we have to infer, because the final performance, that is, the production of fire, would never be possible unless general distinctions as to material, activity, and coördination were kept within the conditions necessary and sufficient for a successful pragmatic performance.

I would like to add here at once that primitive knowledge has yet another factor. When we study present-day savages who still produce fire by friction, make stone implements, and build rudimentary shelters, we can observe that their reasonable behavior, their fidelity to the theoretical principles on which they work, and their technical accuracy are determined by the desired end of their activity. This end is a value in their culture. It is something they appreciate because it satisfies one of their vital requirements. It is a prerequisite of their very existence. This sense of value, however, also pervades and becomes permanently attached to both manual ability and theoretical knowledge. The scientific attitude, embodied in all primitive technology and also in the organization of primitive economic enterprises and social organization, that reliance on past experience with the view to future performance, is an integral factor which must be assumed as having been at work from the very beginning of mankind, ever since the species started on its career as *homo faber,* as *homo sapiens,* and as *homo politicus.* Were the scientific attitude and the valuation of it to become extinct even for one generation in a primitive community, such a community would either lapse into an animal status or, more likely, become extinct.

Thus, out of an inchoate body of environmental factors, random adaptations, and experiences, primitive man in his scientific approach had to isolate the relevant factors and to embody them into systems of relations and determining factors. The final motive or drive in all this was primarily biological survival. The flame of the fire was necessary for warmth and cooking, for safety and for light. Stone implements, shaped and constructed wood, matting and vessels, also had to be produced in order for men to live. All such productive technological activities were based on a theory in which relevant factors were isolated, in which the value of theoretical accuracy was appreciated, in which forethought in achievement was based on carefully formulated experiences from the past.

The main point I am attempting to make here is not so much that primitive man has his science, but first, rather, that the scientific attitude is as old as culture, and second, that the minimum definition of science is derived from any pragmatic performance. Were we to check these conclusions as to the nature of science, drawn from our analysis of the discoveries, inventions, and theories of primitive man, by the advance of modern physics since Copernicus, Galileo, Newton, or Faraday, we would find the same differential factors which distinguish the scientific from other modes of human thought and behavior. Everywhere we find, first and foremost, the isolation of the real and relevant factors in a given process. The reality and relevancy of these factors are discovered by observation or experiment, which establishes their permanent recurrence. Constant empirical verification, as well as the original founding of scientific theory and experience, is obviously of the very essence of science. A theory which fails must be amended by discovering why it has failed. Incessant cross-fertilization of experience and principles is, therefore, indispensable. Science really begins when general principles have to be put to the test of fact, and when practical problems and theoretical relations of relevant factors are used to manipulate reality in human action. The minimum definition of science, therefore, implies invariably the existence of general laws, a field for experiment or observation, and last, but not least, a control of academic discourse by practical application.

It is at this point that the claims of anthropology might be pegged out. This study, for various reasons, has had to converge on the central subject matter in the widest context of all humanistic pursuits, that is, culture. Again, anthropology, especially in its modern developments, has to its credit the fact that most of its votaries have to do ethnographic field-work, that is, an empirical type of research. Anthropology was perhaps the first of all social sciences to establish its laboratory, side by side with its theoretical workshop. The ethnologist studies the realities of culture under the greatest variety of conditions, environmental, racial and psychological. He must be at the same time skilled in the art of observation, that is, in ethnological field-work, and an expert in the theory of culture. In his field-work and in his comparative analysis of culture, he has learned that neither of these two pursuits has any value unless they are carried out conjointly. To observe means to select, to classify, to isolate on the basis of theory. To construct a theory is to sum up the relevancy of past observation and to anticipate empirical confirmation or rebuttal of theoretical problems posed.

Thus, in terms of historical studies, the anthropologist has had to function simultaneously as his own chronicler and as the manipulator of his self-produced sources. In terms of modern sociology, the ethnologist, through his very much simpler task, is able to envisage cultures as a whole and to observe them integrally through personal contact. He has thus provided much of the inspiration towards the really scientific tendencies in modern sociology, the analysis of modern cultural phenomena and direct observation, rather than intuitive, apodeictic armchair revelations. In terms of jurisprudence, economics, politics or the theory of religion, the anthropologist develops the widest inductive evidence for comparison and discrimination.

Thus, it is not as futile, jejune, and presumptuous as it might first appear to discuss the scientific approach to the Study of Man as the real contribution of modern and future anthropology to humanism as a whole. We need a theory of culture, of its processes and products, of its specific determinism, of its relation to basic facts of human psychology and the organic happenings within the human body, and of the dependence of society upon the environment. Such a theory is by no means the monopoly of the anthropologist. He has, however, a special contribution to make, and this may provoke corresponding efforts on the part of the empirically-minded historians, sociologists, psychologists and students of specific type-activities, legal, economic, or educational.

This somewhat pedantic discussion of the scientific quota in social studies needs no apology. There is no doubt that in the present crisis of our civilization we have risen to vertiginous heights in the mechanical and chemical sciences, pure and applied, and in materialistic theory and mechanical engineering. But we have neither faith in, nor respect for, the conclusions of humanistic arguments, nor yet in the validity of social theories. Today we very much need to establish the balance between the hypertrophied influence of natural science and its applications on the one hand, and the backwardness of social science, with the constant impotence of social engineering, on the other. The easy-going flippancy of many a humanist and historian concerning the scientific nature of his pursuits is not merely epistemologically despicable, but in a way immoral, in the pragmatic sense. History and sociology, as well as economics and jurisprudence, must lay their foundations carefully, consciously and deliberately, on the bedrock of scientific method. Social science also must develop into the power of mind used for the control of mechanical power. Humanism will never cease to have its artistic, sentimental and moral elements. But the very essence of ethical principles demands its cogency, and this can only be attained if the principle is as true to fact as it is indispensable to sentiment.

Another reason why I have dwelt so explicitly on the minimum definition of science is because, in an entirely new field of inquiry such as culture, one of the most dangerous procedures is to borrow the methods of one of the older and better established disciplines. Organic similes and mechanical metaphors, the belief that counting and measuring define the line of distinction between science and loose talk—all this and many other tricks of borrowing and leaning upon another discipline have done more harm than good to sociology. Our minimum definition implies that the first task of each science is to recognize its legitimate subject matter. It has to proceed to methods of true identification, or isolation of the relevant factors of its process. This is nothing else than the establishment of general laws, and of concepts which embody such laws. This, of course, implies that every theoretical principle must always be translatable into a method of observation, and again, that in observation we follow carefully the lines of our conceptual analysis. Finally, in all this the inspiration derived from practical problems—such as colonial policy, missionary work, the difficulties of culture contact, and transculturation—problems that legitimately belong to anthropology, is an invariable corrective of general theories.

III CONCEPTS AND METHODS
OF ANTHROPOLOGY

EVEN A BRIEF HISTORY of anthropological achievement would be out of place in this essay. A competent and comprehensive account of all the interests, researches, and theories about exotic peoples and outlandish cultures has still to be written.* There is no doubt that in such a history a great many scientific, as well as antiquarian and sensational sources of inspiration would be discovered in the writings of Herodotus and Tacitus, in the accounts of Marco Polo, of Portuguese and Spanish travellers, and later on, the discoverers and missionaries of the Seventeenth and Eighteenth centuries. The influence of this widening horizon of humanism on some of the French Encyclopaedists deserves special mention.

The accounts of Bougainville and of some of the French Jesuits influenced the theory of the Noble Savage, and inspired Rousseau and Montesquieu, in whose writings we find already two sources of anthropological inspiration: the use of primitive life as a model for civilized man, as well as a criticism of civilization by parallels from savagery. We find there also the more scientific desire to understand culture as a whole by the comparison of its varieties. Montesquieu and Oliver Goldsmith were perhaps the first who attempted a deeper critical understanding of the surrounding culture by comparison with exotic civilizations.

---

* A. C. Haddon's *History of Anthropology* (London, 1934), is brief, but so far the best. T. K. Penniman, *A Hundred Years of Anthropology* (London, 1935), is fuller, but somewhat uninspired. R. H. Lowie, *The History of Ethnological Theory* (New York, 1938), is amusing, colloquial, avowedly partisan, and not always to the point.

Modern anthropology started with the evolutionary point of view. In this it was largely inspired by the great successes of the Darwinian interpretations of biological development, and by the desire of cross-fertilizing prehistoric findings and ethnographic data. Evolutionism is at present rather unfashionable. Nevertheless, its main assumptions are not only valid, but also they are indispensable to the field-worker as well as to the student of theory. The concept of origins may have to be interpreted in a more prosaic and scientific manner, but our interest in tracing back any and every manifestation of human life to its simplest forms remains as legitimate and as indispensable to the full understanding of culture as it was in the times of Boucher de Perthes and J. C. Prichard. I believe that ultimately we will accept the view that "origins" is nothing else but the essential nature of an institution like marriage or the nation, the family or the state, the religious congregation or the organization of witchcraft.

The concept of "stages" remains as valid as that of origins. We would, however, have to make any evolutionary scheme of successive developmental strata either very general or else valid only for certain regions and under certain conditions. Nevertheless, the general principle of evolutionary analysis remains. Certain forms definitely precede others; a technological setting such as expressed in the terms "Stone Age," "Bronze Age," "Iron Age," or the levels of clan or gentile organization, of numerically small groups thinly scattered, as against urban or semi-urban settlements, have to be viewed from the evolutionary point of view in every sound description of a special culture, as well as in any theoretical attempt at comparison, or plotting.

Evolutionism has suffered a temporary eclipse under

the attack of the extreme diffusionist or so-called "historical" schools. For a fair and balanced view I would refer the reader to the article on the subject in the *Encyclopaedia of the Social Sciences*, written by A. A. Goldenweiser. Evolutionism is now the wholly accepted anthropological creed in the Soviet Union, in which form, of course, it ceases to be scientific, and it has been revived in this country in a rational form by several young students, notably A. Lesser and L. White.

The other dominant tendency of older anthropology laid primary stress on diffusion, that is, the process of adopting or borrowing by one culture from another various devices, implements, institutions, and beliefs. Diffusion as a cultural process is as real and unassailable as evolution. It seems certain that no distinction can be made between the two processes. The votaries of either school, however, in spite of their somewhat intransigent and hostile attitude to each other, have approached the problem of culture growth from different angles and have contributed to its illumination independently. The real merit of the diffusionist school consists in their greater concreteness, fuller historical sense, and, above all, in their- realization of environmental and geographical influences. Whether we take the work of Ritter or Ratzel, who probably might be regarded as pioneers of this movement, we find that the correction of the older evolutionism consists in regarding historical processes within the context of the globe. The anthropo-geographic point of view implies, on the one hand, the consideration of each culture within its natural surroundings. As a method it also demands the posing of cultural problems with reference to a map, and to a map of the distribution of cultures in terms of their component parts. In so far as science always gains by moving into another system of determinants, this movement has rendered great services to anthropology.

The rift between evolutionism and diffusionism—and each of them, of course, contains a number of partial schools and divergent opinions—still appears as the main dividing line in method and conceptual outfit. To these two, there is sometimes added at present the functional school, for which the present writer is often held to be largely responsible. In reality, however, and under the magnifying glass of closer scrutiny, we could find a much greater diversity of tendencies, theories, and methods, each characterized by some ultimate conception as to what is the real principle of interpretation; each having some specific approach through which it hopes to reach the comprehension of a cultural process or product; each going into the field with a somewhat differential set of intellectual pigeonholes into which to gather and distribute evidence. Thus there is the comparative method, in which the student is primarily interested in gathering extensive cross-cultural documentations, such as we see in Frazer's *The Golden Bough,* or in Tylor's *Primitive Culture,* or in the volumes of Westermarck on marriage and morals. In such works the authors are primarily interested in laying bare the essential nature of animistic belief or magical rite, of a phase in human culture or a type of essential organization. Obviously, this whole approach presupposes a really scientific definition of the realities compared. Unless we list, in our exhaustive inventories, really comparable phenomena, and are never duped by surface similarities or fictitious analogies, a great deal of labor may lead to incorrect conclusions. Let us also remember that the comparative method must remain the basis of any generalization, any theoretical principle, or any universal law applicable to our subject matter.

Another epistemological device sometimes used exclusively, sometimes completely rejected, is the psychological interpretation of custom, belief, or idea. Thus, Tylor's "minimum definition" of religion, and his whole theoretical concept of animism as the essence of primitive faith and philosophy, is primarily psychological. A host of writers such as Wundt and Crawley, Westermarck and Lang, Frazer and Freud have approached fundamental problems such as origins of magic and religion, of morals and totemism, of taboo and mana, by propounding exclusively psychological solutions. At times the thinker does nothing else but to re-think, in terms of individual armchair philosophy, what the primitive might have or ought to have thought or felt under certain conditions, and how, out of such a thought or feeling, a custom, belief, or practice crystallized. A great Scottish scholar, W. Robertson Smith, was perhaps the first clearly to insist on the sociological context in all discussions which refer not merely to organization of groups but also to belief, to ritual, and to myth. He was followed by the leading French sociologist and anthropologist, Émile Durkheim, who developed one of the fullest and most inspiring systems of sociology. It, however, was marred by certain metaphysical preconceptions and, above all, by the complete rejection not merely of introspective psychological speculations, but also of any reference to the biological basis of human behavior. In many ways, however, Durkheim can be regarded as representing one of the soundest of those tendencies in modern anthropology which aim, above all, at the full scientific understanding of culture as a specific phenomenon.

One or two specific trends or attitudes still have to be mentioned. The words "history" and "historical" have often been used in this essay. I am using these words to describe any process or general development that can be reconstructed in a more or less satisfactory manner, or which has to be assumed as a working hypothesis. In order, however, to make an historical process really significant in terms of explanation or analysis, it is above all necessary to prove that we are, along the time coördinate, linking up phenomena that are strictly comparable. Were it possible to trace the changes in the history of domestic institutions within the same European culture over the space of some five hundred years; were it, moreover, possible to show at each stage how these changes occurred and how they were determined, we could undoubtedly say that we were in the position of a scientifically explanatory history. Even within the realm of recorded history, however, data which would allow us to reconstruct a really scientific history are very scanty, and usually allow, at best, such intelligent and illuminating partial reconstructions as we find in the writings of Taine, Lamprecht, or Max Weber. Once more, as in our criticism of the comparative or diffusionist methods, the value of the results depends on the really scientific definition of the institution which we follow in our inquiry. In anthropological parlance, the terms "history" and "historical" have, so far as I can see, never been satisfactorily defined.

One or two approaches to theoretical anthropology have been born in the dust and welter of an ethnographic museum. The results have, on the whole, been somewhat pernicious. Material objects, as we shall see, play a very specific part in culture. To take an artifact as the model of a cultural element is exceedingly dangerous. The main criticisms which will be made against the *Kulturkreislehre* are directed at the fallacy of taking the physical form of an artifact as the main or exclusive index of cultural identification. Diffusionism, mainly through the influence of certain museum moles like Graebner and Ankermann, has been linked up with the inspiration of ill-assorted and ill-defined objects lumped together in the vitrines and cellars of an old building. Since, however, the basis of diffusionism must be a correct identification of cultural realities plotted on the map, the false identifications derived from the famous criteria of form and quantity have played great havoc with the sound development of that otherwise essentially acceptable tendency.

Somewhat akin to the inspiration from dead objects collected in a museum was the impetus derived from archaeology and prehistory. Here, however, the very environmental setting of the whole problem—its relation to geological stratification; the fact that material traces are often not confined to artifacts only, but contain remains of human beings, related either to life or to death, and also contain traces of vital activities—all this has made the influence of archaeology increasingly stimulating and convergent on the true scientific problem. This undoubtedly centers round the principles on which the archaeologist can reconstruct cultural totalities out of partial remains or traces. Indeed, the whole method of drawing parallels between ethnographic objects and prehistoric findings was inspiring and fruitful, especially in the measure to which the archaeologist and the ethnographer were both interested in those laws of cultural process and product which allow us to relate an artifact to a technique, a technique to an economic pursuit, and an economic pursuit to some vital need of man or of a human group. American archaeology, especially that of the Southwest region, dealing with remains intrinsically related to cultures still in existence, had a more fruitful field and made very good use of it in the brilliant work of Bandelier, and more recently, Gladwin and Haury.

Quite recently the psychoanalytic school brought to the

Study of Man a specific, perhaps one-sided, but important point of view. The anthropologist is perhaps more reserved on the concepts of the "unconscious," "libido," "castration complex," or "the return to the womb" motive. The real contribution of psychoanalysis is its insistence on the formation of mental, that is, also sociological, attitudes during early childhood; within the context of the domestic institution; due to such cultural influences as education, the use of parental authority, and certain primary drives associated with sex, nutrition, and defecation. Indeed, Sigmund Freud somehow succeeded in breaking down our occidental taboo on the various "indecencies," so that anyone using psychoanalytic jargon can now discourse on any matters related to the lower part of the human body, which previously were banned not only from the drawing-room, but also from the academic *aula*. Quite recently, there has developed in the American branch of the psychoanalytic fraternity an emphasis, not to say overemphasis, on cultural influences, which promises a fruitful collaboration between anthropology and the study of the unconscious.* My conviction as to its fertility is due to the fact that the psychoanalysts are bound to search for organic drives as determinants of culture—a position which I have favored since the beginnings of my work in anthropology, and which I elaborated in my article, "Culture," in the *Encyclopaedia of the Social Sciences*. Again, psychoanalysis will never be able to disregard the organic relationship of cultural elements embodied in social groupings. This type of psychology deals with such factors as authority or the use of force, the following up of organic desires and their transformation into values, the study of norms as agencies of repression. All this has already led many adherents of

* *Cf.* the recent book by A. Kardiner and R. Linton, *The Individual and His Society* (New York, 1939).

Freud towards a more-or-less systematic institutional analysis, within which they have placed mental processes.

The approval of psychoanalysis does not in any way detract from the great importance which behaviorism promises to acquire as the basic psychology for the study of social and cultural processes. By behaviorism I mean the newer developments of stimulus-and-response psychology as elaborated by Professor C. Hull at Yale, Thorndike at Columbia, or H. S. Liddell at Cornell. The value of behaviorism is due, first and foremost, to the fact that its methods are identical as regards limitations and advantages with those of anthropological field-work. In dealing with people of a different culture, it is always dangerous to use the short-circuiting of "empathy," which usually amounts to guessing as to what the other person might have thought or felt. The fundamental principle of the field-worker, as well as of the behaviorist, is that ideas, emotions and conations never continue to lead a cryptic, hidden existence within the unexplorable depths of the mind, conscious or unconscious. All sound, that is, experimental psychology can deal only with observations of overt behavior, although it may be useful to relate such observations to the shorthand of introspective interpretation.

The problem as to whether we do or do not admit the existence of "consciousness," "spiritual realities," "thoughts," "ideas," "beliefs," and "values" as subjective realities in other people's minds, is essentially metaphysical. I still see no reason why such expressions referring directly to my own experience should not be introduced, provided that in each case they are fully defined in terms of overt, observable, physically ascertainable behavior. Indeed, the whole theory of symbolism which will be briefly outlined here, consists in the definition of a symbol or idea as something which can be physically recorded, described, or defined. Ideas, thoughts, and emotions have to be treated with all the other aspects of culture, both functionally and formally. The functional approach allows us to determine the pragmatic context of a symbol and to prove that in cultural reality a verbal or other symbolic act becomes real only through the effect which it produces. The formal approach is the basis for our conviction and proof thereof, that in sociological or ethnographic field-work it is possible to define the ideas, the beliefs, the emotional crystallizations of a completely different culture with a high degree of precision and objectivity.

In this rough and rapid survey of the various approaches to anthropological interpretation, of understanding, and of documentation, we have dealt with several categories of exposition and criticism. It is necessary to distinguish clearly between the program, the inspiration, and the leading interest of an evolutionist, as opposed to that of a diffusionist, a psychoanalyst, or a museum mole. The achievements of each school may and must be largely measured by what they set out to do. Again, and at a later stage, a student interested in the history of anthropological thought will be able to put order into these achievements, to delimit the legitimate claims of diffusionism as against evolutionary interpretation; of the sociological one-sidedness of a Durkheim as against the introspective analyses of a Wundt. For the present, we can afford to take a catholic, even eclectic view, and to admit that partly in following their own more or less ambitious programs, partly in elaborating methods, theories, and principles in order to carry out these programs, the schools and tendencies of anthropology have developed an imposing, albeit not completely harmonious structure. Some of the performances, like L. H. Morgan's *Ancient Society,* the fullest and most intransigent exposition of the evolutionary tendencies; W. J. Perry's *Children of the Sun,* an erudite and ambitious exposition of extreme diffusionism; Wundt's seven volumes of *Völkerpsychologie;* Frazer's magnificent comparative corpus, *The Golden Bough,* Westermarck's *The History of Human Marriage*—all these command our respect and admiration.

In this context, however, we are mostly interested in the foundations of the edifice, that is, in the really scientific quota contained in these various works. And here we would probably have to carry out a piece of work partly inspired by the profession of house-wreckers; certainly one in which a great many fundamental points would have to be questioned and one or two persistent errors of method indicated. On the positive side, we would probably give credit to a worker like L. H. Morgan primarily for the discovery of the classificatory system of kinship and for his resolute persistence in studying the principles of primitive relationship by marriage, by blood, and by affinity. In the work of Tylor we would select his pioneering attempt to give a minimum definition of religion, his method of relating causally the relevant factors of human organization, and his ability to distinguish in most of his work the relevant outline of human institutions. Westermarck has contributed more to our knowledge of human marriage and the family by the correct appreciation of such relationships, of the vitality of the domestic institution, and by his penetrating intuitive insight as to the purely ceremonial rôle of various wedding rites, than by his evolutionary linking up of human marriage with the pairing of apes, birds, and reptiles. The specific and permanent contributions of Robertson Smith, of Durkheim, of Freud and his followers, have already been noted.

One school so far unmentioned has generally received less appreciation than it really deserves, perhaps just because of the modesty and scientific limitation of their program. I mean the school of R. S. Steinmetz and his pupils, who perhaps more consistently than anyone else have been satisfied with the scientific analyses of social and cultural fact rather than with more ambitious reconstructive or reinterpretive schemes.

Where do we find the main shortcomings of the various classical schools of anthropology? In my opinion, they always center round the question whether, in constructing an evolutionary stage system, or in tracing the diffusion of this or that cultural phenomenon, the scholar has devoted sufficient attention to the full and clear analysis of the cultural reality with which he deals. Here it would be possible to show that throughout the scores or hundreds of books and articles devoted to primitive marriage, clanship, and kinship, from Bachofen, McLennan, and Morgan, the writings of the German school, either socialistic or juridical, right up to the pretentious three volumes of Robert Briffault, there can hardly be found a single clear analysis of what is meant by a domestic institution or kinship. Indeed, it was here that the opponents of the theory of primitive promiscuity, such as Starcke, Westermarck, Grosse, and Crawley have done much better work as regards the real scientific approach, and their point of view has now been almost universally accepted among all competent modern anthropologists. Again, the main criticism which can be directed against Frazer's valuable analysis of magic is that he concentrated his attention primarily on the rite and formula, and was not sufficiently aware that magic is as magic does. Hence, the ritual performance can not be fully understood except in relation to the pragmatic utilitarian performance in which it is embedded, and to which it is intrinsically related. Tylor's analysis of animism suffers from the fact that he regarded primitive man as a ratiocinating philosopher, forgetting that religion, primitive or civilized, is an active organized effort to remain in touch with supernatural powers, to influence them, and to respond to their biddings.

In all this we can see that not sufficient attention has been given so far to that scientific activity which we described in a previous section, and which consists in clearly defining and relating the relevant factors which operate in such cultural facts as magic, totemism, the clan system, and the domestic institution. It is necessary to show, first and foremost, that a phenomenon which we want to compare in various cultures, which we want to trace in its evolution or follow in its diffusion, is a legitimate isolate of both observation and theoretical discourse. It is necessary to state clearly and precisely where the material determinants, human actions, beliefs and ideas, that is, symbolic performances, enter into such an isolate or reality of culture, how they interact and how they obtain that character of permanent, necessary relationship to each other.

It is obvious that this primary deficiency in theoretical analysis had also a bad influence on field-work. The observer, whether reading such books of instruction and direction as *Notes and Queries,* or inspired by the many and often disagreeing theories, collected isolated items rather than tracing natural, intrinsic, and ever-recurrent relations. It would be an understatement to say that relations between facts and forces are as important as isolated items which stand in these relations to each other. In real science the fact consists in the relatedness, provided that this is really determined, universal, and scientifically definable.

There is, however, one point on which the various older schools have committed a sin of commission, rather than omission. This is the uncritical and, at times, even antiscientific concept of "dead-weights" or cultural fossils in human culture. By this I mean the principle that cultures harbor to a considerable extent, and in positions of strategic importance, ideas, beliefs, institutions, customs, and objects which do not really belong in their context. In evolutionary theories, such dead-weights appear under the guise of "survivals." The diffusionist speaks of them as "borrowed traits" or "trait complexes."

As regards the survival, I quote the definition given by A. A. Goldenweiser, who certainly was not a supporter of evolutionary doctrines. A survival is "a cultural feature which does not fit in with its cultural medium. It persists rather than functions, or its function somehow does not harmonize with the surrounding culture." This is perhaps the best definition of the concept, and the writer who gives it adds, "We know, of course, that survivals exist. They do, in fact, represent a constant and omnipresent aspect of all cultures." With this view I have to disagree. It might be best to discuss the concept with reference to our own culture, which undoubtedly provides more chances for the occurrence of survivals, owing to the vertiginous speed of our present-day progress, than we could find in any other historical situation. Where would we look for survivals? In technological development, the motor vehicle has replaced one drawn by the horse. A horse cart, and even more so, a hansom cab, does not "fit" into the streets of New York or London. Such survivals, however, do occur. The horse cab appears at certain times of the day or night and in certain places. Is it a survival? Yes and no. If we were to treat it as the best and most rapid or cheapest means of locomotion, it certainly would be both an anachronism and a survival. It obviously has changed its function. Does this function fail to harmonize with present-day conditions? Obviously not. Such an antiquated means of locomotion is used for retrospective sentiment, as a "ride into the past"; very often, I am afraid, it moves where the fare is slightly intoxicated or else romantically inclined.

There is no doubt that the survival endures because it has acquired a new meaning, a new function; but unless we adopted some definitely moral or valuational attitude, instead of studying the phenomenon as it now occurs, we would simply give an incorrect description of its uses and its significance. Antiquated types of automobile are never used simply because they have survived, but because people can not afford to buy a newer model. The function is economic. Were we to pass to more important or even national devices or institutions, we could observe that the open fireplace is still prevalent in England and certain parts of France, as against central heating. Here, however, if we drew in the full context of English habits, attitudes, sportive type of life, and attachment to the domestic rôle and convivial influence of an open fire, we will simply have to state that it fulfils a definite rôle in an English house and a New York apartment building.

The real harm done by the concept of survivals in anthropology consists in that it functions on the one hand as a spurious methodological device in the reconstruction of evolutionary series; and, worse than that, it is an effective means of short-circuiting observation in field-work. Take, for instance, Morgan's epoch-making discovery of the classificatory systems of kinship. He regarded them as survivals of a previous evolutionary stage. Considering that he was able to appreciate the extraordinarily near relation between the mode of naming relatives and the organization of the domestic institution, it seems almost incredible that he still asserted that the two were at loggerheads. For, in Morgan's system, we find that the classificatory nomenclature always conveniently survives into the next higher stage, no doubt in order to give the anthropologist the clue to the reconstruction of the previous one. This, however, means in reality that human beings always misrepresented to each other and to the world at large the real kinship conditions round them. In every native society relatives were falsely, or at least inadequately, classified. The old nomenclature survived while new conditions had already arisen. This example of a survival shows, first, that no clear understanding of the rôle of language can be obtained once we continue our dogmatic slumber on the convenient couch of the survival theory. Secondly, such a concept would always stand in the way of any detailed and meticulous field-work aiming at the observation of how the linguistic act of naming is actually related to other activities and interests which constitute the relationship between parents and children, brothers and sisters, kinsmen and clansmen.

Equally destructive has the concept proved in the treatment of marriage ceremonies, as survivals of an older stage in which the symbolism of capture, or purchase or of certain liberties taken toward the bride were conceived of as survivals of previous real modes of contracting marriage. Here also this concept has retarded very much our gradual understanding that the so-called bride-price is never a commercial transaction, but a legal device with complex but perfectly clear and fully obvious economic, juridical, and religious functions. Take any example of "survival." You will find, first and foremost, that the survival nature of the alleged cultural "hangover" is due primarily to an incomplete analysis of the facts. You will also find that most survivals, especially those which have been predicated about important institutions, fundamental elements or usages, have gradually and progressively faded out of anthropological theory. The real harm done by this concept was to retard effective field-work. Instead of searching for the present-day function of any cultural fact, the observer was merely satisfied in reaching a rigid, self-contained entity.

A similar adverse criticism must be applied to the fundamental concept of most diffusionist schools, that of the trait and trait complex. In diffusion, as in any other comparative research, the problem of identity first has to be faced and solved. The credit of having faced this first belongs to F. Graebner, the German museum ethnologist, in his earlier career trained in history, who established the famous and oft-repeated criteria of form and quantity in his pioneering work, *Methode der Ethnologie* (1911). I have challenged this methodological device as fundamentally unscientific, and as basing the whole discipline of diffusionism on an anti-scientific foundation, in the article s. v. "Anthropology," in the thirteenth edition of the *Encyclopaedia Britannica,* as follows:

The extreme representative of the diffusionist school, Graebner, maintains that all the regularities of cultural process are "laws of mental life" and that "their scientific and methodical study is possible only from the psychological point of view" (Graebner, p. 582, 1923), while Pater Schmidt, Wissler, Lowie and Rivers constantly use psychological interpretations. Thus, no anthropologist nowadays wishes completely to eliminate the study of mental processes, but both those who apply psychological explanations from the outset and those who want to use them after culture has been "historically analysed" forget that interpretation of culture in terms of individual psychology is as fruitless as mere historical analysis; and that to dissociate the studies of mind, of society and of culture, is to foredoom the results.

As influential and one-sided as the psychological trend is the interpretation of similarities and analogies of culture by the principle of mechanical transmission. First vigorously propounded by Ratzel as the main problem of ethnology, the study of distribution and diffusion has been followed up by Frobenius, Ankermann, Graebner, Pater W. Schmidt, Pater Koppers and subsequently by the late Dr. Rivers. Whether the doctrines recently propounded by Prof. Elliot Smith and Mr. Perry about the universal spread of culture from Egypt will have to be classed with other discarded hypotheses or whether they contain a permanent contribution to the history of culture remains to be seen. Their use of anthropological data is unsatisfactory * and their argument really belongs to archaeology, in which field their views have met with adverse criticism.† One or two competent anthropologists, however, have given these theories their vigorous support (Rivers, C. E. Fox).

The merit of the moderate anthropological diffusionism lies in its geographical rather than in its historical contributions. As a survey of facts correlated to their geographical substratum, it is a valuable method of bringing out the influence of physical habitat as well as the possibilities of cultural transmission. The distributions mapped out for America by Boas, Spinden, Lowie, Wissler, Kroeber, Rivet and Nordenskiöld; the survey of Melanesian cultures given by Graebner; of Australian provinces given by W. Schmidt; of Africa prepared by Ankermann, will possess lasting value.

The historical hypotheses of Frobenius, Rivers, Schmidt and Graebner, the sweeping identifications of "culture complexes" all over the globe, will not so easily pass muster. They suffer from a lifeless and inorganic view of culture and treat it as a thing which can be preserved in cold storage for centuries, transported across oceans and continents, mechanically taken to pieces and recompounded. Historical reconstructions within limited areas, such as have been done upon American material

* A. A. Goldenweiser, *Early Civilization*, p. 311; R. H. Lowie, *Amer. Anthrop.*, pp. 86-90 (1924); B. Malinowski, *Nature* (March 11, 1924).

† O. G. S. Crawford, *Edinburgh Review*, pp. 101-116 (1924); T. D. Kendrick, *Axe Age*, p. 64 *et seq.* (1925); J. L. Myres, *Geographical Teacher*, No. 71, pp. 3-38 (1925); Presidential Address, *Folk-Lore*, XXXVI, 1925, p. 15; Flinders Petrie, *Ancient Egypt*, pp. 78-84 (1923); T. E. Peet, *Journal of Egyptian Archaeology*, vol. 10, p. 63 (1924); A. M. Blackman, *ibid.*, pp. 201-209.

for instance, in so far as they are based on definite records or on archaeological evidence, give results which can be empirically verified, hence can be of scientific value. Dr. B. Laufer's study on the potter's wheel and certain contributions to the history of American culture (T. A. Joyce, A. V. Kidder, N. C. Nelson, H. J. Spinden, L. Spier) are methodologically acceptable, though they belong to archaeology rather than to the science of living races and cultures. Such sound works must be clearly distinguished from the productions in which a conjectural history is invented *ad hoc* in order to account for actual and observable fact, in which therefore the known and empirical is "explained" by the imaginary and unknowable.[*]

Quite recently a new and very competent revival of trait analysis has been undertaken at the University of California. Professor A. L. Kroeber, the leader of this inquiry, quite rightly recognizes that trait analysis and the characterization of culture by traits or trait complexes depends on the question whether they can be isolated as realities, and thus made comparable in observation and theory. Here I shall quote the relevant argument:

"Are our elements or factors, the culture traits, independent of each other? While we are not prepared to answer this question categorically, we believe that culture traits are in the main if not in absolutely all cases independent.[†] This is because so many of them have been shown over and over again, in all domains of culture

[*] Quoted by permission of the publishers, Encyclopaedia Britannica, Inc.

[†] Within the limits of ordinary logic or common sense. Essential parts of a trait cannot of course be counted as separate traits: the stern of a canoe, the string of a bow, etc. Even the bow and arrow is a single trait until there is the question of an arrowless bow. Then we have two traits, the pellet bow and the arrow bow. Similarly, while the sinew backing of a bow cannot occur by itself, we legitimately distinguish self-bows and sinew-backed bows; and so, single-curved and recurved bows, radically and tangentially feathered arrows, canoes with blunt, round, or sharp sterns, etc.

and in all parts of the world, to occur at times dissociated even if at other times or places they are frequently or even preponderantly associated,* that it becomes a fair inference, until contrary cases are demonstrated, that all traits can occur independently of each other. That, at any rate, appears to be the implicit assumption of all anthropologists of the last generation, with the exception of the few survivors of the Tylor-Morgan-Frazer 'evolutionistic' school, and possibly the group of functionalists.† If then we are in error on this point, we believe that nine-tenths of the anthropology and culture history practiced today is also in error in a fundamental if generally unexpressed assumption; and in that case a general inquiry on this point is in order."

I am deeply convinced that there is a fundamental misunderstanding in any attempt at isolation of separate traits. Indeed, the positive contribution of this essay will show how far and under what conditions we can isolate relevant realities, and where the treatment of traits or trait complexes is inadmissible. This will obviously not be an attempt to substitute one word or phrase for another. Those who prefer to use such words as trait and trait complex, instead of speaking of institutions, organized groups, artifacts in use, or beliefs and ideas insofar as they pragmatically affect human behavior, are quite welcome to retain any labels or verbal usages. The only point which matters is whether we are able to isolate a related set of phenomena on the basis of a really scientific analysis, or on a mere arbitrary assumption. And again, the real point is whether, following Graebner, we

---

* Thus baptism occurs without confession in certain Christian sects or denominations.

† The assumption seems to underlie the work of students as diverse in their methods as Boas, Ratzel, Rivers, Elliot Smith, Wissler, Graebner, Schmidt, Lowie, Dixon, Rivet, etc.

attach the maximum value to characteristics of a trait or the composition of a complex, insofar as they are extrinsic and irrelevant; or whether, on the contrary, we look only for relations and for forms which are determined by the cultural forces really at work. The second is the only scientific way to our understanding of what culture really is. The first, which is directly opposed to it, can not, therefore, be scientific. On this point there can be no compromise, and there is no middle way.

IV   WHAT IS CULTURE?

AT THE OUTSET it will be well to take a bird's eye view of culture, in its various manifestations. It obviously is the integral whole consisting of implements and consumers' goods, of constitutional charters for the various social groupings, of human ideas and crafts, beliefs and customs. Whether we consider a very simple or primitive culture or an extremely complex and developed one, we are confronted by a vast apparatus, partly material, partly human and partly spiritual, by which man is able to cope with the concrete, specific problems that face him. These problems arise out of the fact that man has a body subject to various organic needs, and that he lives in an environment which is his best friend, in that it provides the raw materials of man's handiwork, and also his dangerous enemy, in that it harbors many hostile forces.

In this somewhat casual and certainly unpretentious statement, which will be elaborated piece by piece, we have implied first that the theory of culture must take its stand on biological fact. Human beings are an animal species. They are subject to elemental conditions which have to be fulfilled so that individuals may survive, the race continue and organisms one and all be maintained in working order. Again, in his whole outfit of artifacts and his ability to produce them and to appreciate them, man creates a secondary environment. There is nothing new said so far, and similar definitions of culture have often been stated and elaborated. We shall, however, draw one or two additional conclusions.

36

In the first place, it is clear that the satisfaction of the organic or basic needs of man and of the race is a minimum set of conditions imposed on each culture. The problems set by man's nutritive, reproductive, and hygienic needs must be solved. They are solved by the construction of a new, secondary, or artificial environment. This environment, which is neither more nor less than culture itself, has to be permanently reproduced, maintained, and managed. This creates what might be described in the most general sense of the term as a new standard of living, which depends on the cultural level of the community, on the environment, and on the efficiency of the group. A cultural standard of living, however, means that new needs appear and new imperatives or determinants are imposed on human behavior. Clearly, cultural tradition has to be transmitted from each generation to the next. Methods and mechanisms of an educational character must exist in every culture. Order and law have to be maintained, since coöperation is the essence of every cultural achievement. In every community there must exist arrangements for the sanctioning of custom, ethics, and law. The material substratum of culture has to be renewed, and maintained in working order. Hence, some forms of economic organization are indispensable, even in the most primitive cultures.

Thus man has, first and foremost, to satisfy all the needs of his organism. He has to create arrangements and carry out activities for feeding, heating, housing, clothing, or protection from cold, wind, and weather. He has to protect himself and organize for such protection against external enemies and dangers, physical, animal, or human. All these primary problems of human beings are solved for the individual by artifacts, organization into coöperative groups, and also by the development of knowledge, a sense of value and ethics. We shall attempt to show that a theory can be developed in which the basic needs and their cultural satisfaction can be linked up with the derivation of new cultural needs; that these new needs impose upon man and society a secondary type of determinism. We shall be able to distinguish between instrumental imperatives—arising out of such types of activity as economic, normative, educational and political—and integrative imperatives. Here we shall list knowledge, religion, and magic. Artistic and recreational activities we shall be able to relate directly to certain physiological characteristics of the human organism, and also to show their influence and dependence upon modes of concerted action, magical, industrial, and religious belief.

If such an analysis discloses to us that, taking an individual culture as a coherent whole, we can state a number of general determinants to which it has to conform, we shall be able to produce a number of predictive statements as guides for field-research, as yardsticks for comparative treatment, and as common measures in the process of cultural adaptation and change. From this point of view culture will not appear to us a "patchwork of shreds and tatters," as it has been quite recently described by one or two competent anthropologists. We shall be able to reject the view that "No common measure of cultural phenomena can be found," and that "The laws of cultural processes are vague, insipid, and useless."

The scientific analysis of culture, however, can point to another system of realities that also conforms to general laws, and can thus be used as a guide for field-work, as a means of identification of cultural realities, and as the basis of social engineering. The analysis just outlined, in which we attempt to define the relation between a cultural performance and a human need, basic or derived, may be termed functional. For function can not be defined in any other way than the satisfaction of a need by an activity in which human beings coöperate, use artifacts, and consume goods. Yet this very definition implies another principle with which we can concretely integrate any phase of cultural behavior. The essential concept here is that of *organization*. In order to achieve any purpose, reach any end, human beings have to organize. As we shall show, organization implies a very definite scheme or structure, the main factors of which are universal in that they are applicable to all organized groups, which again, in their typical form, are universal throughout mankind.

I propose to call such a unit of human organization by the old but not always clearly defined or consistently used term, institution. This concept implies an agreement on a set of traditional values for which human beings come together. It also implies that these human beings stand in definite relation to one another and to a specific physical part of their environment, natural and artificial. Under the charter of their purpose or traditional mandate, obeying the specific norms of their association, working through the material apparatus which they manipulate, human beings act together and thus satisfy some of their desires, while also producing an impression on their environment. This preliminary definition will have to be made more precise, more concrete, and more cogent. But here again, I wish primarily to insist that unless the anthropologist and his fellow humanists agree on what is the definite isolate in the concrete cultural reality, there will never be any science of civilization. And here also, if we achieve such an agreement, if we can develop some universally valid principles of institutional action, we shall once more lay a scientific foundation for our empirical and theoretical pursuits.

Obviously, neither of these two schemes of analysis implies that all cultures are identical, nor yet that the student of culture must be more interested in identities or similarities than he is in differences. I submit, however, that in order to understand divergencies, a clear, common measure of comparison is indispensable. It will, moreover, be possible to demonstrate that most of the divergencies which are often attributed to specific national or tribal genius—and that not only in the theory of National Socialism—are the reason for institutions organized around some highly specialized need or value. Such phenomena as head-hunting, extravagant death-rituals and ways of burial, and magical practices, can be best understood as the local elaboration of tendencies and ideas essentially human but especially hypertrophied.

Our two types of analysis, functional and institutional, will allow us to define culture more concretely, precisely and exhaustively. Culture is an integral composed of partly autonomous, partly coördinated institutions. It is integrated on a series of principles such as the community of blood through procreation; the contiguity in space related to coöperation; the specialization in activities; and last but not least, the use of power in political organization. Each culture owes its completeness and self-sufficiency to the fact that it satisfies the whole range of basic, instrumental and integrative needs. To suggest, therefore, as has been recently done, that each culture only covers a small segment of its potential compass, is at least in one sense radically wrong.

Were we to plot out all the manifestations of every culture in the world, we obviously would find such elements as cannibalism, head-hunting, couvade, potlatch, kula, cremation, mummification, and a vast array of detailed peripheral eccentricities. From this point of view obviously no single culture covers all the itemized freaks and eccentricities of many others. Yet this approach, I submit, is essentially unscientific. It fails, first and foremost, to define, on the principles of relevancy, what can be regarded as the real and significant elements of a culture. It fails also to give us any clue, in comparing some of these apparently exotic "isolates," to customs or culture arrangements in other societies. As a matter of fact, we shall be able to show that some realities which seem very strange at first sight are essentially cognate to very universal and fundamentally human cultural elements; and this very recognition will admit of the explanation, that is, the description in familiar terms, of exotic customs.

It will also be necessary, of course, to introduce the element of time, that is, of change. Here we shall attempt to show that all evolutionary or diffusion processes happen, first and foremost, in the form of institutional change. Whether in the form of invention, or as an act of diffusion, a new technical device becomes incorporated into an already established system of organized behavior, and produces gradually a complete remolding of that institution. Again, in terms of our functional analysis, we will show that no invention, no revolution, no social or intellectual change, ever occurs except when new needs are created; and thus new devices in technique, in knowledge, or in belief are fitted into the cultural process or an institution.

This brief outline, which is really a blueprint for our following fuller analysis, indicates that scientific anthropology consists in a theory of institutions, that is, a concrete analysis of the type units of an organization. As a theory of basic needs, and a derivation of instrumental and integrative imperatives, scientific anthropology gives us the functional analysis, which allows us to define the form, as well as the meaning, of a customary idea or contrivance. It can easily be seen that such a scientific approach does not by any means override or deny the validity of evolutionary or historical pursuits. It simply supplies them with a scientific basis.

V THEORY OF
ORGANIZED BEHAVIOR

THE ESSENTIAL FACT of culture as we live it and experience it, as we can observe it scientifically, is the organization of human beings into permanent groups. Such groups are related by some agreement, some traditional law or custom, something which corresponds to Rousseau's *contrat social*. We always see them coöperating within a determined material setting: a piece of environment reserved for their use, an equipment of tools and artifacts, a portion of wealth which is theirs by right. In their coöperation they follow the technical rules of their status or trade, the social rules of etiquette, customary deference, as well as religious, legal, and moral customs forming their behavior. It is always possible also to define and determine sociologically what effect the activities of such an organized human group produce, what need they satisfy, what services they render to themselves and the community as a whole.

It will be well to make this general statement plausible by a brief empirical reference. Let us first consider under what conditions private initiative becomes a cultural fact. The invention of a new technological device, the discovery of a new principle, or formulation of a new idea, a religious revelation or a moral or æsthetic movement, remain culturally irrelevant unless and until they become translated into an organized set of coöperative activities. The inventor has to take out a patent and form a company for the production of his new device. He has, therefore, first and foremost to convince some people that his invention will pay to be industrialized, and then other people will have to be convinced that the article is worth purchasing. A company has to be formed and chartered, capital has to be procured, techniques developed, and then the industrial campaign is launched. This consists of productive, commercial, and advertising activities that may succeed or fail, in other words, may fulfil a definite economic function in satisfying a new need, after this has been created, as in the case of radio, or else in satisfying more successfully an old need, as in innumerable products such as artificial silk, Nylon, more effective cosmetics or a new brand of whiskey.

In the same way a new revelation, such as the one which occurred to Mrs. Mary Baker Eddy or to Mrs. Aimee Semple MacPherson or Joseph Smith or Frank Buchman, has, first and foremost, to be brought home to a group of people. They then organize, that is, equip themselves materially, and adopt a number of rules of status and rules of performance, with which they carry out their ritual activities and practice their dogmatic and moral principles. They thus satisfy a set of spiritual needs, less basic no doubt than those related to artificial silk fabrics or a brand of whiskey, but nevertheless real. A scientific discovery has also to be embodied and documented through the material apparatus of a laboratory, observational reference or statistical documentation, as well as the printed word. It has to convince a number of people. It has to be applied practically, or at least related to other branches of knowledge, and then it can be said to have fulfilled the specific scientific function of having increased our knowledge. If we were to examine from this point of view any movement, such as Prohibition or birth control, fundamentalism or nudism, a committee for the promotion of race relations or an organization like the Bund, the Ku Klux Klan, or Father Coughlin's

Social Action, we would see that in one and all we can register a certain agreement on the statement of a common purpose as between the members of the movement. We would also have to study the organization of such a movement with regard to leadership, rights of property, division of functions and activities, duties and benefits derived. We would have to register the technical, ethical, scientific, and legal rules or by-laws governing the behavior of the group; it would be well to check such rules as against the actual performances of the people. Finally, we would have to assess the position of such a group with relation to the community as a whole, that is, to define its function.

True to our principles, we have started from our own civilization, convinced that anthropology might as well begin at home. We also started by analyzing whether any idea, principle, device, religious revelation, or moral principle has any social or cultural relevancy without being organized. Our answer was clearly in the negative. A point of view, an ethical movement, the greatest industrial discovery, are culturally null and void, so long as they are confined to the head of one person. Had Hitler developed all his racial doctrines, all his visions of a Nazified Germany and of a world enslaved to its rightful owners, the German Nazis; had he massacred all the Jews, Poles, Hollanders, or English people and carried out the conquest of the world—had he done all this in his head only, the world would have been happier and the science of culture and of savagery deprived of one of its most monstrous, albeit most illuminating examples of how private initiative, falling on fertile soil, can lead to universal disaster and world-wide bloodshed, famine, and corruption. We could make similar statements in a different vein about the discoveries of Isaac Newton, about the plays of Shakespeare, about the ideas of Mohammed or St. Francis or of the founder of Christianity himself. Neither history nor sociology nor anthropology is concerned with what happens and remains within the skull of an individual, however much there may be contained in it of genius, of vision, of inspiration, or of malignity. Hence the general principle here developed, that the science of human behavior begins with organization.

There are, however, types of concerted activities which are not due to the implementation of individual initiative within the historical movement in which they occurred. Every human being is born into a family, a religion, a system of knowledge, and often into a social stratification and political constitution, which, often having existed for ages beforehand, are not changed or even affected during his lifetime. Let us, therefore, supplement our previous analysis and look around us, indeed follow our own destinies in a day of work or in the history of a lifetime. We shall, again, find that everywhere and in every effective performance the individual can satisfy his interests or needs and carry out any and every effective action only within organized groups and through the organization of activities. Consider your own existence or that of any one of your friends or acquaintances. The individual goes to sleep and wakes up in his home, in a hostel, in a camp, or in some "institution," whether it be Sing Sing, a monastery, or a residential college. Each of these represents a system of organized and coördinated activities in which service is given and taken, in which a material shelter with the minimum of comforts, or the maximum, is provided, which is run at a certain expense and paid for, which contains an organized group of people who administer it and which has a set of rules, more or less codified, which the inmates have to follow.

The organization of all and each of these institutions, whether domestic, residential, or correctional, is based on a constitutional law, on a set of values and agreements. Each of them also satisfies a set of needs of the inmates and of society at large, and thus fulfills a function. Unless we deal with a monastery or Sing Sing, the individual, after he has waked, performs the indispensable sanitary activities and ablutions, eats his morning meal, and issues forth. He proceeds then to a place of business, or else carries out some shopping or hawks about his wares or ideas in some form of salesmanship. In every case his activities are determined by his relation to some commercial or industrial business, to a school or a religious institution, to a political association or a recreational organization of which he is the official or the servant. If we were to survey the daily behavior of any individual, male or female, young or old, healthy or sick, we would find that all phases of his existence must be related to one or other of the systems of organized activities into which our culture can be subdivided; which, in their agglomerate, really constitute our culture. Home and business, residence and hospital, club and school, political headquarters and church, everywhere we find a place, a group, a set of by-laws, and rules of technique, and also a charter and a function.

A fuller analysis would show, moreover, that in each case we have a very definite objective foundation for our analysis, in the study of the environmental setting with the specific objects which belong there, the buildings, the equipment, and the capital sunk into an institution. We would also find that to understand an athletic club or a scientific laboratory, a church or a museum, we would have to become acquainted with the rules, legal, technical and administrative, that coördinate the activities of the members. The personnel who run any of the here-mentioned institutions have to be analyzed as an organized group. This means we would have to state the hierarchy, the division of functions, and the legal status of each member, as well as his relations to the others. The rules or norms, however, invariably are worded so as to define the ideal behavior. The checking of this ideal with reference to actual performance is one of the most important tasks of the anthropologist or sociologist engaged in scientific field-work. Hence, in our analysis, we would always distinguish clearly and explicitly the rules or norms from the activities.

The organization of each such system of activities also implies the acceptance of certain fundamental values and laws. It is always the organization of people for a given purpose, accepted by themselves, and recognized by the community. Even were we to consider a gang of criminals, we would see that they also have their own charter defining their aims and purposes, while the society as a whole, especially in its organs of law and order, recognizes such an organization as criminal, that is, as dangerous and one to be detected, uprooted, and punished. Thus, once more, it is clear that the charter, that is, the recognized purpose of the group, and the function, that is, the integral effect of the activities, have to be clearly distinguished. The charter is the idea of the institution as entertained by its members and defined by the community. The function is the rôle of that institution within the total scheme of culture, as defined by the investigating sociologist in a primitive or developed culture.

In short, if we wanted to give a description of individual existence in our own civilization or in any other, we would have to link up its activities with the social scheme of organized life, that is, with the system of institutions prevailing in that culture. Again, the best description of any culture in terms of concrete reality would consist in the listing and analysis of all the institutions into which that culture is organized.

I submit that this type of sociological approach is the one which *de facto* has been, though as a rule somewhat implicitly, practiced by historians, by students of economics, politics, or any other branch of social science, in their assessment of cultures and societies. The historian has very largely dealt with political institutions. The economist, of course, is concerned with institutions organized for the production, marketing, and consumption of goods. Those who have dealt with the history of science or of religion, or given us comparative analyses of systems of knowledge and of belief, were also primarily dealing, more or less successfully, with phenomena of human knowledge and faith as organized entities. Nevertheless, in treating what is usually called the spiritual aspects of civilization, the sober and substantial approach in terms of social organization has not always been recognized. Histories of philosophic thought, of political ideology, of discovery, or of artistic creation, have only too often neglected the fact that any form of individual inspiration can only become wholly a cultural reality if it can capture the public opinion of a group, implement the inspiration with material means of its expression, and thus become embodied into an institution.

The economist, on the other hand, sometimes is apt to underrate the fact that while systems of production and of property do unquestionably determine the whole range of the manifestations of human life, they in turn are determined by systems of knowledge and of ethics. In other words, the extreme Marxian position, which would regard the economic organization of a system as the final determinant of culture, seems to underestimate two cardinal points in the analysis here presented: first, the concept of charter, by which we find that any system of production depends upon the knowledge, the standard of living defined by the whole range of cultural factors, and the system of law and political power; second, the concept of function, by which we see that distribution and consumption are as much dependent upon the total character of a culture as on the productive organization itself. In other words, the analysis here propounded would definitely urge that within each specific universe of discourse of any social discipline, a considerable degree of cross-fertilization with other aspects of cultural reality ought to be practiced, in order to avoid hypostasis and a search for first or true causes.

Were we to pass from our own culture to any other less known and more exotic one, we would find exactly the same conditions. The Chinese civilization differs from ours in the organization of family life and its relation to ancestor worship; in differences of their village and municipal structure; in the existence of an extensive clan system; and, of course, also in the economic and political organization of the country. Studying an Australian tribe, we would have to follow the small family groups, the hordes into which the families cluster, the marriage classes, the age-grades, and totemic clans. A description of each such unit would assume significance and become comprehensible only if we related the social organization to its material setting; if we were able to collect the code of rules obtaining within each group, and, again, show how this is derived by the natives from some general principles which invariably have a legendary, historical, or mythological background of precedent and primeval revelation. In relating the general types of activities, and their effects on the total life, we would be able to assess the function of each system of organized activities, and thus show how conjointly they provide the natives with food and with shelter, with order and training, with systems of environmental orientation, and with beliefs by which these people place themselves in harmony with the general destiny of their life. The student of the higher and more primitive civilizations of the large Asiatic peninsula of India would analyze the caste system in relation to Brahminism, and the monasteries derived from the tenets of Buddhistic faith. By observation of village communities, of crafts, markets, and industrial enterprise, he would gradually come to understand and be able to explain how these natives derived their livelihood from their environmental resources.

Thus, in primitive and civilized communities alike, we see first and foremost that all effective human action leads to organized behavior. We begin to perceive that this organized behavior can be submitted to a definite analytic scheme. We probably have perceived that the type of such institutions, or isolates of organized behavior, presents certain fundamental similarities throughout the wide range of cultural variety. We can now, therefore, proceed to an explicit, almost diagrammatic definition of the concept of institution, which is, I submit, the legitimate isolate of cultural analysis.

VI THE CONCRETE ISOLATES
OF ORGANIZED BEHAVIOR

IN ORDER TO MAKE the foregoing analysis more definite and more serviceable in field-work and in theory, it will be best to represent it in a diagrammatic form, to give clear definitions of the various concepts we have derived from it, and to supplement it with as full and concrete a list of universally valid types as possible. The concept we have been elaborating is that of an organized system of purposeful activities. We have stated, first and foremost, that human beings are born or enter into already formed traditional groups. Or else, at times they organize or institute such groups. I shall define as the charter of an institution the system of values for the pursuit of which human beings organize, or enter organizations already existing. The personnel of an institution I shall define as the group organized on definite principles of authority, division of functions, and distribution of privileges and duties. The rules or norms of an institution are the technical acquired skills, habits, legal norms, and ethical commands which are accepted by the members or imposed upon them. It is clear already, perhaps, that both the organization of the personnel and the nature of the rules followed are definitely related to the charter. In a way both the personnel and the rules are derived from, and contingent upon, the charter.

An important fact has been registered throughout oui analysis: all organization is invariably based upon and intimately associated with the material environmental setting. No institution is suspended in the air or floating in a vague, indefinite manner through space. One and all have a material substratum, that is, a reserved portion of the environmental outfit in wealth, in instruments, and also a portion of the profits accruing from concerted activities. Organized on the charter, acting through their social and organized coöperation, following the rules of their specific occupation, using the material apparatus at their disposal, the group engages in the activities for which they have organized.

The distinction between *activities* and *rules* is clear and precise. The activities depend on the ability, power, honesty, and good-will of the members. They deviate invariably from the rules, which represent the ideal of performance, not necessarily its reality. The activities, moreover, are embodied in actual behavior; the rules very often in precepts, texts, and regulations. Finally, we have introduced the concept of function, that is, the integral result of organized activities, as distinguished from charter, that is, the purpose, the traditional or new end to be obtained. The distinction is essential.

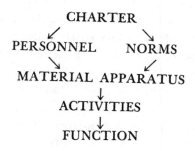

The diagram here presented gives a concrete, mnemonic illustration of this argument. It is not to be regarded as a mystical *eidos* or a magical talisman. It is merely one way of relating, in a condensed manner, the results of the present analysis, and of impressing on mind and memory the relationship between the various points which we have set apart in the present analysis. It is also meant to show quite clearly that every type of effective activity has to be organized in one way and one way only, through which it becomes culturally stabilized, that is, incorporated into the cultural heritage of a group.

The results of our analysis, however, as embodied in the diagram, are definitely ambitious. The diagram stands for the following propositions. Each institution, that is, organized type of activity, has a definite structure. In order to observe, understand, describe, and discourse theoretically upon an institution, it is necessary to analyze it in the manner here indicated, and in this manner only. This applies to field-work and to any comparative studies as between different cultures, to problems of applied anthropology and sociology, and indeed, to any scientific approach in matters where culture is the main subject matter. No element, "trait," custom, or idea is defined or can be defined except by placing it within its relevant and real institutional setting. We are thus insisting that such institutional analysis is not only possible but indispensable. It is maintained here that the institution is the real isolate of cultural analysis. It is also maintained that any other type of discussion or demonstration in terms of isolated traits or trait complexes, other than those which would follow the institutional integration, must be incorrect.

In order, however, to demonstrate even more fully that the institutional structure is universal throughout all cultures, and within each cultural manifestation, it will be best to supply first another broad but important generalization. I submit that although even institutions such as the family, state, age-group or religious congregation vary as between one culture and another and, in some cases, within the same culture, it is possible to draw up a list of types or classes representative of any and every culture. In other words, I would maintain that the family, and the type of activities based on a permanent marriage contract in which reproduction, education, and domestic coöperation are the dominant interests, can be listed as a cultural universal. Let us attempt to construct such a list. This might be conceived as a useful device for any field-worker going out to some previously unstudied savage or civilized area, and intent upon tracing, observing, and recording all the relevant types of organized behavior. Such a list would also be a useful measure in comparative research, whether oriented on evolutionary, diffusionist or historical lines. It would also constitute proof that in a certain sense each culture has to cover the groundwork of concrete and organized purposeful combinations of human beings into established activity-groups.

In order to construct such a list it might be best to consider the general principles which bind human beings together and integrate them into permanent groups. We have, of course, first and foremost, the fact of reproduction. In all human societies, reproduction, that is, the relationship between husband and wife, and parents and children, leads to the formation of small yet exceedingly important groups. We can, therefore, speak about the reproductive principle of integration or the principle of kinship, that is, relationship by blood and relationship by marriage. Under this heading we would have to list such institutions as the family, including the contract of marriage, rules of descent, and laws of domestic organization. The bonds of parenthood, that is, the reciprocal relationship between parents and children, are always extended, and they lead to the formation of extended kindred groups. These either consist of agglomerations of individual families under the authority of a patriarch or matriarch, or else in the formation of so-called classificatory kinship groups, usually designated by such terms as clan, sib, gens, or phratry. There are, as is well known, a great many distinctions as between matrilineal and patrilineal descent, matrilocal and patrilocal marriage, the dual system, the multiple coupled clan system, and so on and so forth. In spite of the various controversies as to the "origins" of marriage and the family, about the real significance of clanship and the linguistic and other manifestations of classificatory kinship systems, the fact remains that no competent field-worker can study a tribe without being well acquainted with the general theory of primitive family life, the law of descent and kinship, and the formation of extended groups of relatives. We might, therefore, note in a kind of condensed shorthand, that under the reproductive principle of social integration, the law of marriage, descent and kinship, with all its consequences for the social structure, has to be studied.

Another general principle of grouping is that of propinquity and contiguity. The essence of social life is coöperation. People can only exchange services, work together, and rely on supplementing each other as regards task and ability, when they are within reach. And conversely, people who are close neighbors must come to some agreement on a whole number of points. They must delimit their rights of residence, their use of objects of general interest and utility. They have sometimes to act conjointly when some danger, calamity, or pressing business calls them to action. Obviously the smallest neighborhood group is the household, so that this series starts with the same institution as the one discussed above. Yet invariably we have also some forms of organization which embrace a number of families and other kinship units. The local group may consist of a nomadic horde, a sedentary village, a little municipality or township, or be simply the organization of scattered hamlets or homesteads. Since there are, however, as pointed out above, definite advantages in organization, while lack of organization is impossible, because it would leave a whole set of burning questions unsolved, it is always possible to determine the institution which we might call *municipality* in the widest sense of the term, or the local group. The principle of propinquity, like that of kinship, can be extended several removes. Here a much greater latitude prevails, and according to the situation, we might speak of areas, districts, provinces, all or one of them, always bearing in mind that we can list them as institutions only insofar as they are definitely organized. The widest such territorial unit of potential coöperation, exchange of services, and community of interest would be the tribe, in the cultural sense of the term.

Another natural principle of distinction and of integration is that connected with human physiology and anatomy. In this human beings differ as regards sex, age, and, far less significantly, as regards certain innate stigmata, deficiencies, or pathological conditions. Whenever an organization is established which unites all males to the exclusion of all females, we could say that we have institutionalized sex groups. This usually occurs as a by-product of other activities. Even in primitive tribes there is a collective division of functions as between men and women. Very rarely only, as, for instance, in some Australian tribes, do we have a clear-cut division into male and female totemic clans. More frequently the organization according to sex is related to the other system here listed, that of age groupings or age-grades. This phenomenon is very widely distributed and, in a certain sense, is universal. It is universal from the most primitive culture up to our modern Western civilization, in that certain stages of human life are marked out, and to these stages there correspond periods of complete dependence upon the social milieu, as in infancy and, to a certain extent, in childhood; the period of training and learning; the period of adolescence as between sexual maturity and marriage; the period of full tribal membership; and finally, the stage of senility. This latter may either be associated with great influence in tribal or national affairs, for which an ethnographic word, gerontocracy, has been coined; or else it simply means that old men and old women are allowed to vegetate virtually outside the full current of tribal life. In some cultures physical and mental abnormalities, such as sexual inversion or epileptic or hysterical tendencies, form the basis of group organization, at times connected with shamanism, at times constituting a partially outlawed caste.

The principle of association, that is, voluntary grouping by individual initiative, must be distinguished from the principles already enumerated. Membership in secret societies, in clubs, and in recreational teams or artistic fraternities, depends on this principle. Here again, we have a type of institutional phenomenon which can be discovered, at least in rudimentary forms, even among most primitive peoples, and which runs up through all evolutionary stages, being as pronounced in our own culture as among the Polynesians and West African Negroes. Here, as in the system of age-grades above described, we have very often a system of initiation rites, often an economic by-play, at times strictly secret and mysterious, or at times open and public.

The fifth principle of integration of great importance, which increases with the evolution of humanity, is that by occupational ability, training, and preference. This, clearly, is a far less specific type, because the distinctions as regards occupation, training, and differentiation of typical activities vary more from culture to culture than differences in reproductive or territorial necessities. Here, however, we would find invariably in all cultures occupational institutions connected with the production, distribution, and consumption of food and other goods. We would find, thus, coöperative teams among the simplest food gatherers, among hunters, fishermen, and agriculturists. We would find magical and religious congregations such as the totemic clan, the kinship group engaged in ancestor worship, and the tribe as a whole or its subdivisions worshipping a nature divinity. Very often sorcerers and witches are organized into professional groups, either in reality or in the traditional belief of the tribe.

It is clear that, as culture advances, the various occupational and specific functional tasks become gradually differentiated and incorporated into specific institutions. Education must exist among the lowest primitives; indeed, as the transmission of traditional techniques, values, and ideas, it must have existed from the very beginning of humanity. But it is incorporated into the family, the local group, the association of playmates, the age-grade, and the economic guild of craftsmen where the novice receives his apprenticeship. Special institutions for the training of the young, that is, schools, colleges, and universities, are one of the newest acquisitions of humanity. In the same way true knowledge and, indeed, science, are present at the earliest stages of culture. Organized research becomes institutionalized only at the very highest levels of development. And so it is with law and with industrial production, charitable institutions

and professions such as medicine, teaching, trade union-
ism, and engineering. At very low cultural levels, we have
mostly rudimentary economic, magico-religious, artistic
and recreational groups dependent on early forms of
specialization.

The distinction by status and rank, the formation of
class and caste, do not occur at the earliest levels of
culture. But they occur with the development of wealth,
of military power, of conquest, and thus, of ethnic stratification. In the latter sense, we might even have introduced the principle of race as one which can become
institutionalized, as in the castes of India, in the two or
three-layer societies of the Sudan and East Africa, and,
to a certain extent, in the various racial discriminations
and counter-measures in our own society.

If we were now to inquire how and on what principles
these various institutions are integrated into definite,
self-contained wholes, an important distinction would
have to be made. An ethnographic survey of the world
demonstrates that on every continent there are well-
defined boundaries which separate, one from the other,
units or cultural entities which we anthropologists call
tribes. In this sense the unity of such a geographically
defined group consists in the homogeneity of culture.
Within the boundaries of the tribe the writ of the same
culture runs from end to end. The tribesmen all speak the
same language, hence accept the same tradition in mythology and customary law, in economic values and in moral
principles. With this there runs parallel a similarity of
techniques and implements, of tastes and consumers' goods.
They fight, hunt, fish, and till the soil with the same
type of implements and weapons, and they intermarry
according to the same tribal law of matrimony and
descent. Hence, the members of such a group can com-

municate by word; they can interchange services, and they can be mobilized for a common enterprise. Whether we can consider such a culturally unified group—which, in fact, is the prototype or antecedent of a nation in the modern sense—as an institution, may be left open. It is probably better to describe the nation, primitive or civilized, as an integral of partly autonomous, but also interdependent institutions. In this, nationality means unity in culture.

There is, however, one more principle of integration thus far omitted. I mean the principle of authority, in the full sense of the term. Authority means the privilege and the duty of making decisions, of pronouncing in cases of dispute or disagreement, and also the power of enforcing such decisions. Authority is the very essence of social organization. Hence, it can not be absent from any single institutional organization. There are, nevertheless, institutions which are primarily integrated on the use of effective force. We could define them as political institutions, and speak about a political coefficient or quota in the family, municipality, the province, or even an economic or religious team. The real importance, however, of this principle begins with the development of military organizations, and with their use in aggression and defence. The tribe as a cultural unit probably existed long before the political tribe became organized on the principle of force. Among the Australian aborigines or among such people as the Veddas, the Firelanders, the Pygmies, and the Andamanese, we can not speak of the political organization of the tribe, since this does not exist. In many somewhat more developed communities, in Melanesia and among the Polynesian-speaking Oceanians, the political group or the prototype state is found usually associated with the sub-division of the tribe. At a more advanced stage we have the two units coinciding, and we can then speak of a prototype of the nation-state.

However this may be, it would be well to draw the distinction between the tribe as a cultural unit and the tribe as a political organization. The latter is definitely a form of institution which has to be defined in all the points into which we analyze the concept, and which are represented in our diagram. And it would be always important to make quite clear how far it does or does not coincide with the cultural group.

It will be well to condense this analysis into a brief list:

LIST OF UNIVERSAL INSTITUTIONAL TYPES

Principle of Integration

1. Reproduction
   (*Bonds of blood defined by a legal contract of marriage and extended by a specifically defined principle of descent on the genealogical scheme.*)

Types of Institution

The family, as the domestic group of parents and children.

Courtship organization.

The legal definition and organization of marriage as a contract binding two individuals and relating two groups.

The extended domestic group and its legal, economic, and religious organization.

Groups of kindred united on the unilateral principle of descent.

The clan, matrilineal or patrilineal.

The system of related clans.

2. Territorial
   (*Community of interests due to propinquity, contiguity, and possibility of coöperation.*)

The neighborhood group of municipalities, such as the nomadic horde, the roaming local band, the village, the cluster of hamlets or homesteads, the town, the city.

The district, the province, the tribe (Cf. 7).

3. Physiological
   (*Distinctions due to sex, age, and bodily stigmata or symptoms.*)

Primitive sex totemic groups.

Organizations based on physiological or anatomical sex distinctions.

Organizations due to sexual division of functions and activities.

Age groups and age-grades, insofar as they are organized.

Organizations in primitive societies of the abnormal, the mentally deranged, the epileptics (often connected with magical or religious ideas); at higher levels, institutions for the sick, the insane, the congenitally defective.

4. Voluntary Associations

Primitive secret societies, clubs, recreational teams, artistic societies.

At higher levels, the clubs, mutual aid and benefit societies, lodges, voluntary associations for recreation, uplift, or the realization of a common purpose.

5. Occupational and Professional

   (*The organization of human beings by their specialized activities for the purpose of common interest and a fuller achievement of their special abilities.*)

At a primitive level, primarily of magicians, s o r c e r e r s, shamans, and priests; also guilds of craftsmen and economic teams.

As civilization develops, the innumerable w o r k s h o p s, guilds, and undertakings, economic interest groups, and associations of professional workers in medicine, in law, in teaching, and in ministering to religious needs.

Also specific units for the organized exercise of teaching (schools, colleges, universities); for research (laborat o r i e s, academies, institutes) ; for administration of justice (legislative bodies, courts, police force); for defence and aggression (army, navy, air force); for religion (parish, sects, churches).

6. Rank and Status

Estates and orders of nobility, clergy, burghers, peasants, serfs, slaves. The caste system.

Stratification by ethnic, that is, either racial or cultural distinctions at primitive and developed levels.

7. Comprehensive

   (*The integration by community of culture or by political power.*)

The tribe as the cultural unit corresponding to nationality at more highly developed levels.

The cultural sub-group in the regional sense or in the sense of small enclaves (a l i e n minorities, the ghetto, the gypsies.)

The political unit which may comprise part of the tribe or its totality or yet include several cultural subdivisions. The distinction bet w e e n tribe-nation and tribe-state as a political organization is fundamental.

This list summarizes the argument of the present section. As it stands, it obviously is a fairly commonsense statement, indicating that certain general types of organization are to be found in every culture. From the point of view of ethnographic observation, such a list has a predictive value to the student, in that it forces the observer to answer positively or negatively a series of questions, all of which must be made clear if we want to have a full characterization of a culture not yet studied.

It will be well, perhaps, to restate the theoretical import of this list once more. It declares in its left-hand column, first and foremost, that reproduction, distribution by territory, physiological distinctions, occupational distinctions, one and all produce definite types of grouping, and that each type of grouping has the same general structure which we predicated in our concept of institution. It also affirms that voluntary associations, whether in the form of secret societies or clubs or other purposeful groupings, are universally to be found, and that the manner in which the widest coöperative group is integrated on the principle of cultural homogeneity and political power is essential to our knowledge of a community. The entries on the left-hand side enumerate a set of universal problems, which are solved by each culture in a somewhat different manner. And it is the solution of these problems, that is, the function of the various institutional types, that provides the primary determinism. This, again, however, will have to be still expanded. It is clear that, while reproduction represents a fundamental determinant in each society, the territorial principle is formal, indicating that, given certain vital interests to be pursued in common, a spatial setting is necessary, primarily because people must be in reach of one another in order to coöperate. We shall have, therefore, to study more fully the vital interests that bind a group to its territory. We also have to understand more fully how these specific occupational interests arise, and how they are related to the basic requirements of human life and group existence.

We need, in short, a fuller statement of our theory of basic needs, of the derivation of cultural interests, and of the environmental, social, and technical determinants of all instrumental, collective, and coöperative behavior. Only after a fuller discussion of these problems, in which the concept of function will be clarified, shall we be able to return to the present list and to establish more convincingly that our institutional types are not arbitrary or fictitious, but represent clearly definable realities.

THE FUNCTIONAL ANALYSIS
OF CULTURE

IT IS CLEAR that if we want to live up to our definition of science, it will be necessary to answer a number of questions posed rather than solved by our previous analysis. In the concept of institution, as well as in the assertion that each special culture can be analyzed into institutions, and also that all cultures have as their main common measure a set of institutional types, there are already implied a number of generalizations or scientific laws of process and of product.

What still remains to be made clear is the relation between form and function. We have insisted that each scientific theory must start from and lead to observation. It must be inductive and it must be verifiable by experience. In other words, it must refer to human experiences which can be defined, which are public, that is, accessible to any and every observer, and which are recurrent, hence fraught with inductive generalizations, that is, predictive. All this means that, in the final analysis, every proposition of scientific anthropology has to refer to phenomena which can be defined by form, in the fullest objective sense of the term.

At the same time, we also indicated that culture, as the handiwork of man and as the medium through which he achieves his ends—a medium which allows him to live, to establish a standard of safety, comfort, and prosperity; a medium which gives him power and allows him to create goods and values beyond his animal, organic endowment—that culture, in all this and through all this, must be understood as a means to an end, that is, instrumentally or functionally. Hence, if we are correct in both assertions, a clearer definition of the concept of form, of function, and of their relations, must be given.

Right through our analysis, we have seen that man changes the physical environment in which he lives. We asserted that no organized system of activities is possible without a physical basis and without the equipment of artifacts. It would be possible to show that no differential phase in any human activity occurs without the use of material objects, artifacts, consumers' goods—in short, without the incidence of elements of material culture. At the same time there is no human activity, concerted or individual, which we could regard as purely physiological, that is, "natural" or untutored. Even such activities as breathing, the work of internal secretions, digestion, and circulation happen within the artificial environment of culturally determined conditions. The physiological processes within the human body are affected by ventilation, by the routine and range of nutritive processes, by conditions of safety or danger, of satisfaction or anxiety, of fear or hope. In turn, such processes as breathing, excretion, digestion, and the ductless glands affect culture more or less directly, and give rise to cultural systems referring to the human soul, to witchcraft, or to metaphysical systems. There is a constant interaction between the organism and the secondary milieu in which it exists, that is, culture. In short, human beings live by norms, customs, traditions, and rules, which are the result of an interaction between organic processes and man's manipulation and re-setting of his environment. We have here, therefore, another cardinal constituent of cultural reality: whether we call it norm or custom, habit or *mos,* folkway or usage, matters little. I shall, for the sake of simplicity, use the term *custom* to cover all traditionally regulated and standardized forms of bodily behavior. How can we define this concept, so as to make clear its form, hence open the scientific approach to it, and relate this form to the function?

Culture, however, includes also some elements which apparently remain intangible, inaccessible to direct observation, and where neither form nor function is very evident. We speak more or less glibly about ideas and values, about interests and beliefs; we discuss motive in folk tales, and dogmatic conceptions in the analysis of magic or religion. In what sense can we speak of form when we approach the belief in one God, or the concept of *mana,* or the tendency toward animism, preanimism, or totemism? Some sociologists resort to the hypothesis of a collective censorium, hypostatize Society as "the objective moral being, which imposes its will upon its members." It is clear, however, that nothing can be objective which is not accessible to observation. Most scholars who deal with the analysis of magic or religion, primitive knowledge or mythology, are satisfied with description in terms of introspective individual psychology. Here, once more, we can never obtain a final decision between one theory and another, between one assumption or conclusion and its contrary, by the appeal to observation, since obviously we can not observe the mental processes of the savage, or, for that matter, of anyone else. We have, therefore, once more the task of defining the objective approach to what might be roughly described as the spiritual quota in culture, and also indicate the function of idea, belief, value, and moral principle.

It probably is clear by now that the problem we are facing here, and trying to elaborate with a certain amount of thoroughness, perhaps even pedantry, is the fundamental problem of each science: the establishment of identity of its phenomena. That this problem still awaits its solution, and that the science of culture still lacks real criteria of identification—that is, criteria of what to observe and how to observe, what to compare and how to carry it out, of what to trace in evolution and diffusion —will hardly be disputed by anyone acquainted with the controversies of history, sociology, or anthropology. In this latter science, there is one school whose members base most of their researches on and around the concept of heliolithic culture. Those who reject such theories would flatly deny that heliolithic culture is a reality which can be identified all over the globe. They would dispute the identification carried out with reference to megalithic monuments, dual organization, the elephant's trunk symbol, the interpretation of the sexual symbolism in the cowrie shell, in fact, every one of the realities postulated.

Within the functional school, to take an example nearer home, there is dispute as to whether the principal functional explanation must revolve about the fact of "social density," the solidarity of the group, its integration, and such phenomena as euphoria and disphoria, which are held to be unidentifiable by one branch of functionalists and real by the other. Whereas most anthropologists agree that the family, at least, is a real isolate of cultural reality that can be identified and traced throughout humanity, and is a universal of all culture, there are still not a few anthropologists who dispute the identity of this cultural configuration or institution. Most anthropologists are satisfied that totemism does exist. The late A. A. Goldenweiser, in a brilliant essay published in 1910, an essay which, in my opinion, marks a milestone in the development of anthropological method, questioned the identity of totemism. In other words, he challenged those who write about this phenomenon, and trace its origins, its development, and its diffusion, to prove that in observation and in theoretical discourse we can treat totemism as a legitimate isolate.

Thus, the task of establishing the criteria of identification, both in field-work and in theory, and also in speculation, hypothesis and applied anthropology, is perhaps the most important contribution towards making the Study of Man scientific. Let me approach this question from the elementary problem of the field-worker. When he first takes his residence among people whose culture he wishes to understand, to record, and to present to the world at large, he obviously is faced with the question of what it means to identify a cultural fact. For, clearly, to identify is the same as to understand. We understand the behavior of another person when we can account for his motives, his drives, his customs, that is, his total reaction to the conditions in which he finds himself. Whether we use introspective psychology, and say that understanding means identification of the mental processes, or whether, as behaviorists, we affirm that his response to the integral stimulus of the situation follows lines familiar to us from our own experiences, does not change the argument profoundly. Ultimately and as a principle of method in field-work, I would insist on the behavioristic approach, because this allows us to describe facts which can be observed. It remains true, however, that in current and intuitive practice we react and respond to the behavior of others through the mechanism of our own introspection.

And here a very simple but too often neglected principle occurs at once. The actions, material arrangements, and means of communication which are most directly significant and comprehensible are those connected with man's organic needs, with the emotions, and with practical methods for satisfying needs. When people eat or rest, when they obviously are attracted to each other or engaged in courtship, when they warm themselves at a fire, sleep on a bunk, when they fetch food and water in order to prepare a meal, we are not puzzled, we have no difficulty in giving a clear account or bringing home to members of a different culture what is really happening. The unfortunate result of this basic fact is that anthropologists have followed their untrained predecessors and neglect somewhat those elemental phases of human existence, just because they seem to be obvious and generally human, non-sensational and non-problematic. And yet it is clear that a selection made on the principle of exotic, sensational or outlandish divergencies from the universally human run of behavior is in itself not a scientific selection, because the most ordinary satisfactions of elementary human needs are very relevant to all organized behavior.

It would be easy to show that the historian also invariably uses as the basis of his reconstruction the physiological argument that all human beings have to live not by bread alone, but primarily by bread; that every army must get along on its stomach and, probably, also most large-scale organizations; that in short, as in the phrase of the famous story, history can be condensed into the statement, "They lived, they loved, they died." *Primum vivere, deinde philosophari;* the principle that people can be kept quiet by the wise ministration of bread and circuses; the comprehension, that is, that there is a system of needs, some fundamental, others maybe artificially developed, but all craving for satisfaction—all such phrases and principles constitute the historian's stock-in-trade of wise, albeit intuitive reconstruction. It is clear, I think, that any theory of culture has to start from the organic needs of man, and if it succeeds in relating the more complex, indirect, but perhaps fully imperative needs of the type which we call spiritual or economic or social, it will supply us with a set of general laws such as we need in sound scientific theory.

When is it that the field-worker in anthropology, the theoretical scholar, the sociologist and the historian feel that it is necessary to supply an explanation by hypotheses, by ambitious reconstruction or by a psychological assumption? Obviously, when human behavior begins to appear strange and unrelated to our own needs or customs, where, in short, human beings cease to behave as all human beings would, and carry out their practices of couvade, of head-hunting, of taking scalps, of worshipping a totem, an ancestor, or a strange god. It is characteristic that many of these customs belong to the realm of magic, of religion, and that they are due, or appear so, to deficiencies in primitive knowledge or reason. The less directly organic the need to which human behavior refers, the more likely it will breed those phenomena which have provided the greatest amount of food for anthropological speculation. But this is only partly true. Even with reference to eating, sex, and to the growth and decay of the human body, there exist a number of problematic, exotic, and strange types of behavior. Cannibalism and food taboos; marriage and kinship customs; hypertrophied sexual jealousy or an apparently complete absence of it; classificatory terms of kinship and their disregard of physiological paternity; finally, the extraordinary confusion, diversity, and contradiction in burial custom and eschatological ideas form another large body of culturally determined behavior, which seems to us, at first sight, strange and incomprehensible. Here, obviously, we deal with phenomena in which a very strong emotional reaction inevitably occurs. All that relates to human nutrition, to sex, and to the cycle of life, including birth, growth, maturation, and death, is invariably surrounded by physiological disturbances in the body, in the nervous system of the participant and his associates. This, once more, suggests to us that if we want to approach the difficulties and complexities of cultural behavior, we have to relate them to organic processes in the human body and to those concomitant phases of behavior which we call desire or drive, emotion or physiological disturbance, and which, for one reason or another, have to be regulated and coördinated by the apparatus of culture.

There is one point referring to surface comprehensibility which we left out in this part of our discussion. Obviously there is a whole area of human behavior which has to be specifically learned by the field-worker and brought home to the comprehending reader, and that is the specific symbolism of each culture, primarily language. This, however, refers directly to the problem which we have already posed, namely, that of defining the symbolic function of an object, a gesture, an articulate sound, which must be related to the general theory of needs and their cultural satisfaction.

VIII WHAT IS HUMAN NATURE?
(The Biological Foundations of Culture)

WE HAVE TO BASE our theory of culture on the fact that all human beings belong to an animal species. Man as an organism must exist under conditions which not only secure survival, but also allow of healthy and normal metabolism. No culture can continue if the group is not replenished continually and normally. Otherwise, obviously, the culture will perish through the progressive dying out of the group. Certain minimum conditions are thus imposed on all groups of human beings, and on all individual organisms within the group. We can define the term "human nature" by the fact that all men have to eat, they have to breathe, to sleep, to procreate, and to eliminate waste matter from their organisms wherever they live and whatever type of civilization they practice.

By human nature, therefore, we mean the biological determinism which imposes on every civilization and on all individuals in it the carrying out of such bodily functions as breathing, sleep, rest, nutrition, excretion, and reproduction. We can define the concept of basic needs as the environmental and biological conditions which must be fulfilled for the survival of the individual and the group. Indeed, the survival of both requires the maintenance of a minimum of health and vital energy necessary for the performance of cultural tasks, and for the minimum numbers necessary for the prevention of gradual depopulation.

We have already indicated that the concept of need is merely the first approach to the understanding of organ-

75

ized human behavior. It has been several times suggested that not even the simplest need, nor yet the physiological function most independent of environmental influences, can be regarded as completely unaffected by culture. Nevertheless, there are certain activities determined biologically, by the physics of the environment and by human anatomy, which are invariably incorporated in each type of civilization.

Let me present this in a diagrammatic form. In the adjoining table a series of vital sequences are listed. Each of them has been analyzed into a tripartite concatenation of phases. There is an impulse which is primarily determined by the physiological state of the organism. We find there, for instance, a state of the organism which would occur if breathing were temporarily prevented. We all know what this feeling is from personal experience. The physiologist can define it in terms of biochemical processes in the tissues, in terms of the function of circulation, the construction of the lungs, and the processes of oxidation and carbon monoxide. The impulse or appetite connected with digestive processes can also be stated in terms of human psychology formulated by introspection or personal experience. Objectively, however, this can be referred for its scientific statement to the physiologist, more specifically to the dietitian and specialist in digestive processes. A textbook on the physiology of sex can define the appetite of this instinct by reference to human anatomy and the physiology of reproduction. The same obviously refers to fatigue, which is an impulse to stop, for the time being, muscular and nervous activity; to bladder and colon pressure, and also perhaps to somnolence, to the impulse to move, so as to exercise muscles and nerves, and the impulse to avoid direct organic dangers, such as impact or falling down a precipice or a height. The avoidance of pain is perhaps a general impulse related to the avoidance of danger.

PERMANENT VITAL SEQUENCES INCORPORATED IN ALL CULTURES

(A) *Impulse→*	(B) *Act→*	(C) *Satisfaction*
Drive to breathe; gasping for air	intake of oxygen	elimination of CO_2 in tissues
hunger	ingestion of food	satiation
thirst	absorption of liquid	quenching
sex appetite	conjugation	detumescence
fatigue	rest	restoration of muscular and nervous energy
restlessness	activity	satisfaction of fatigue
somnolence	sleep	awakening with restored energy
bladder pressure	micturition	removal of tension
colon pressure	defecation	abdominal relaxation
fright	escape from danger	relaxation
pain	avoidance by effective act	return to normal state

In the second column we list the physiological performance corresponding to each impulse. This perhaps is the least variable in the series as regards any cultural influences or motivation. The actual intake of air or food; the act of conjugation; sleep, rest, micturition, or defecation, are phenomena which can be described in terms of anatomy, physiology, biochemistry, and physics. More correctly, perhaps, we might say that a minimum definition in objective anatomical and physiological terms can be given for each process, although even here certain cultural modifications occur.

In the last column we list the end-results of physiological activities, in their relationship to the original impulse. Here, once more, we find that, through the activities listed in the middle column, a change occurs in the human body, producing very definite conditions in the tissues which introspectively are felt as easing up, relief, satisfaction. In terms of observable behavior we would have to define them as organic quiescence, as a return to the normal chronic activities, as in breathing, or the resumption of other tasks as in the case of evacuation. In the case of the sexual impulse, we have here the condition generally described by psychologists and physiologists as detumescence.

It has to be noted, however, that here conjugation, that is, the essential performance of the instinct, and the temporary quiescence of both organisms concerned, is under certain conditions only the starting point of another biological process of primary importance. Effective conjugation engenders the process of pregnancy in one of the two organisms. Here we have a complex biological sequence of events, in which a new organism comes into being, at first within the maternal body, later on separating in the act of birth and starting a partly independent career of ontogenic development. The process of growth, intra-uterine and later on individual, also is a biological fact associated with a variety of impulses and needs, and has to be listed as a biological determinant of culture. Here, however, we can not place growth under the heading of impulse, although growth definitely implies a series of additional impulses, especially in infancy, and is definitely related to the appearance of certain impulses at different stages of development. We shall briefly discuss this later when we define the relation between impulse or drive and need.

This argument aims at establishing the meaning of the expression "human nature." We have shown that biological determinism forces upon human behavior certain invariable sequences, which must be incorporated into every culture, however refined or primitive, complex or simple. We have already emphasized the fact that all three phases occur in every culture, and that their concatenation is as permanent and non-variable, as is the minimum physiological nature of every phase. Each of these tripartite vital sequences is indispensable to the survival of the organism, and, as regards sexual conjugation and pregnancy, to the continuation of the community. It is clear that the anatomical, biological, and physical aspects of these processes are not primarily the concern of the science of culture. It is necessary, however, for the student of culture to lay stress on this essentially physiological basis of culture. For reasons theoretical and practical, anthropology, as the theory of culture, must establish a closer working coöperation with those natural sciences which can supply us with the specific answer to our problems. Thus, for instance, in the study of various economic systems connected with the production, distribution, and consumption of food, the problem with which the dietitian or physiologist of nutrition is concerned is fundamentally linked up with anthropological work. The nutritive specialist can define the optimum of a diet in terms of proteins, carbohydrates, mineral salts and vitamins necessary for the maintenance of the human organism in good health. This optimum, however, must be defined with reference to a given culture. For the optimum is only definable with relation to the amount of labor, muscular and nervous, to the complexity of tasks, to potential strains and efforts demanded by a given cultural configuration from its members. At the same time, the ideal formula provided by a dietitian is of no practical or theoretical importance unless we can relate it to environmental supplies, to the systems of production and possibilities of distribution.*

I am here summing up the type of research with which I was connected for several years in the work of the International Institute of African Languages and Cultures. When African labor is drafted into European enterprise, whether mines, plantations, or factories, it is usually found that the workers are undernourished with reference to the efforts which they will have to put into their performances. It has also been discovered by specialized work among the various African tribes that under new strains arising from culture change in general, their food supply, sufficient in the past, becomes inadequate. Thus, even in practical and applied anthropology the analysis here submitted has passed out of the stage of mere desideratum and into the stage of actual research.

The theoretical importance, however, of the problem would lead to a slightly different interchange of question and answer as between the biologist and the student of culture. It would be of the greatest importance for our comparative study of organized human behavior if we could learn from those who study comparative human anatomy and physiology and the environmental setting of these, what are the limits within which human organisms may remain in satisfactory working order in terms of

---

* Studies of this problem have been made by Dr. A. I. Richards, Dr. Margaret Read, Dr. Raymond Firth, and Lord Hailey.

intake of food, supply of oxygen, range of temperature, amount of moisture in the air or directly reaching the skin—that is, the minimum conditions of physical environment compatible with growth, metabolism, protection from micro-organisms, and sufficient reproduction. On this last point, for instance, the great problem of depopulation, the more or less rapid dying out of some primitive races and cultures and of survival of others, is a question which scientific anthropology can not shirk. Here probably mere gynecological studies or even a purely physiological theory of reproduction would not be sufficient. The relations between the whole organism and especially the happenings within the nervous system, and the "will to live" and "will to reproduce" is a question which has been opened by such students as G. H. Lane-Fox Pitt-Rivers and a few physical anthropologists, but it still awaits solution.

As regards the present analysis, however, we only need to state that the vital sequences summed up in our table have to be defined biologically in the first place. They are related to culture primarily through the re-definition of impulses, and also through the fact that the satisfaction of an impulse, or as some behaviorists would say, the reinforcement of a drive, is a constant psychological and physiological factor which controls human behavior throughout the vast range of traditionally determined activities. We shall be able to see clearly that the whole vast areas of highly complicated and differentiated cultural activities, at primitive and at highly developed levels, are one and all related more or less directly to the vital sequences here enumerated. This, of course, is not a new idea. Indeed, one or two of the most influential systems of cultural philosophy or of general interpretation of human behavior, in terms of one dominant principle,

have selected one or the other of our vital sequences
and have attempted to show that it is the prime mover of
humanity as a whole. The Marxian system implies that
the hunger→ feeding→ satiation series is the ultimate
basis of all human motivation. The materialistic interpretation of history stresses partly the fundamental need
of nutrition, partly the importance of material culture,
that is, wealth, especially in its productive phase. Sigmund
Freud and his followers extended the drive which we
modestly listed as sex appetite into a somewhat metaphysical concept of the libido, and attempted to account for most
phases of social organization, ideology, or even economic
interests by infantile fixations of libidinous drives. In this
process they also included the activities of the colon and
bladder, and thus reduced the prime movers of humanity
to the regions and processes occurring just below the
human waist. The fact, however, remains that the human
organism is anatomically and physiologically differentiated, and the autonomy of the various impulses has to
be sustained. Each drive commands a specific type of
performance, and each vital sequence is to a large extent
independent of others.

As regards the problem of form and function, it will
be possible to show that we can already define both at
this level of analysis. Each of our vital sequences has its
definite form. Each can be described in terms of anatomy,
physiology and physics. And the minimum statement of
what effective behavior, induced by a drive and leading
to a satisfaction, has to be, a statement made in terms of
natural science, is the definition of the form of such a
vital sequence. As regards function, this to the physiologist
is primarily the relation between the conditions of the
organism before the act, the change brought about and
leading to the normal state of quiescence and satisfaction.

Function, in this simplest and most basic aspect of human behavior, can be defined as the satisfaction of an organic impulse by the appropriate act. Form and function, obviously, are inextricably related to one another. It is impossible to discuss the one without taking account of the other. In breathing, for instance, the "form" as regards the human body might appear as the intake of air. But if the surrounding atmosphere has an insufficiency of oxygen, or is filled with monoxide or some other poisonous gas, the effect would be very different from the intake of fresh air. Could we say here that the same form presents a different function? Obviously not. In our definition of form we have included not merely the central act of the vital sequence, but also the initial condition of the organism, the environmental setting, and the final result of the act, in terms of what happens to the organism in its interaction with environmental factors. When some poisonous gas reaches the lungs, the form of the microphysiological processes is obviously different from that of oxidation. In other words, we would have here a difference in function, because the form of the process as a whole was changed. The form here, in terms of overt behavior, would represent not the organism breathing for some time, and then reaching the state of normal satisfaction due to the renewal of oxygen in the tissues but the state of collapse, radically different as regards the total activity and the condition of the tissues. We could say that the formal approach corresponds to the method of observation and documentation in the statement of a vital sequence, while function is the restatement of what has happened in terms of scientific principles drawn from physics, biochemistry, and anatomy, that is, a full analysis of organic and environmental happenings. It is legitimate to distinguish the two concepts since they correspond to different methods of observation and operational devices. It is impossible to omit either of the two in the analysis of human behavior as it is expressed in any one of the vital sequences enumerated in our table.

The anthropologist who has to study the impulses not in their minimum definition supplied by physics and biology, but as phases of organic behavior incorporated into culture, has to redefine the two concepts of form and function, and to him both assume an additional complexity and also a less self-evident value and utility.

IX THE DERIVATION OF
CULTURAL NEEDS

So FAR WE have learned that human nature imposes on all forms of behavior, however complex and highly organized, a certain determinism. This consists of a number of vital sequences, indispensable to the healthy run of the organism and to the community as a whole, which must be incorporated in each traditional system of organized behavior. These vital sequences constitute crystallizing points for a number of cultural processes, products, and complex arrangements which are built around each sequence. We were also about to see that the concepts of form and function have already been defined with reference to a vital sequence as a mere organic performance.

Let us now consider how impulses, activities, and satisfactions actually occur within a cultural setting. As for the impulse, it is clear that in every human society each impulse is remolded by tradition. It appears still in its dynamic form as a drive, but a drive modified, shaped, and determined by tradition. In the case of breathing, this occurs within enclosed spaces, a house, a cave, a mine, or a factory. We could say that there is a compromise between the need for oxygen in the lungs and the need for integral protection during sleep, work, or social gathering. The requirements of temperature and of ventilation have to be met by cultural devices. In this a certain traditional adjustment or habituation of the organism takes place. It is a well-known fact that even in European cultures, the emphasis on fresh air as against level of temperature is not identical in England, Germany, Italy and Russia. Another complication in this simple impulse of air intake to fill the lungs with oxygen is due to the fact that the organs of breathing are also, to a large extent, organs of speech. A compromise, an adjustment of deep breathing to performances in public oratory, the recital of magical formulae, and singing, constitutes another domain in which cultural breathing differs from the mere physiological act. The interaction between beliefs, magical, religious, and connected with etiquette, and breathing, would supply another co-determinant to that of physiology in cultures where the exhalation of breath, especially at close quarters, is regarded as dangerous, impolite, or noxious, while the deep, noisy intake of breath is a sign of respect or submission.

Cultural determination is a familiar fact as regards hunger or appetite, in short, the readiness to eat. Limitations of what is regarded as palatable, admissible, ethical; the magical, religious, hygienic and social taboos on quality, raw material, and preparation of food; the habitual routine establishing the time and the type of appetite—all these could be exemplified from our own civilization, from the rules and principles of Judaism or Islam, Brahminism or Shintoism, as well as from every primitive culture. The sex appetite, persistent and invariably allowed within limitations, is also hedged round by the strictest prohibitions, as in incest, temporary abstinences, and vows of chastity, temporary or permanent. Celibacy obviously eliminates—at least as an ideal demand—the sexual relations from certain minorities within a culture. As a permanent rule, it clearly never occurs for a community as a whole. The specific form in which the sexual impulse is allowed to occur is deeply modified by anatomical inroads (circumcision, infibulation, clitoridectomy, breast, foot, and face lacerations); the attractiveness of a sex object is affected by economic status and rank; and the integration of the sex impulse involves the personal desirability of a mate as an individual and as a member of the group. It would be equally easy to show that fatigue, somnolence, thirst, and restlessness are determined by such cultural factors as a call to duty, the urgency of a task, the established rhythm of activities. Similar factors obviously also affect bladder and colon pressure and impulses of pain and fear. As for pain, indeed, it would seem that most of the elementary invariants of cultural history and ethnographic data prove that resistance and endurance can be almost indefinitely increased by changes in the central system achieved through religious enthusiasm, the heroism of a patriot, or the model determination of a Puritan.

In short, it would be idle to disregard the fact that the impulse leading to the simplest physiological performance is as highly plastic and determined by tradition as it is ineluctable in the long run, because it is determined by physiological necessities. We see also why simple physiological impulses can not exist under conditions of culture. Breathing has somehow to be combined with vocal performances, with confinement within the same space of several people, and activities in which air is affected by noxious or poisonous gases. Eating, under conditions of culture, is not the mere resort to environmental supplies, but something in which human beings partake of prepared food which, as a rule, has been for some time accumulated and stored, and which invariably is the result of an organized differential activity of a group, even when this occurs in the simplest form of collecting. Eating in common implies conditions as to quantity, habit, and manner, and thus derives a number of rules of commensalism. Conjugation in the human species is not an act to be performed anywhere, anyhow, without consideration of the feelings or reactions of others. Conjugation in public is, in fact, extremely rare, and occurs either as a direct deviation from the norms of the society as a form of sexual perversion, or, very rarely, as a part of a complex magical or mystical ceremony. In such cases, it becomes rather the cultural use of a physiological fact than a biologically determined satisfaction of a mere impulse. The act of resting, sleep, of muscular or nervous activity, and the satisfaction of restlessness, invariably demand a specific setting, a physical apparatus of objects, and special conditions arranged and allowed for by the community. In the simplest, as well as in highly complex civilizations, micturition and defecation are performed under very special conditions and are surrounded by a rigid system of rules. Many primitives, for reasons of magic and in fear of sorcery, as well as because of their ideas of dangers emanating from human excreta, impose stricter rules of privacy and isolation than we find even in civilized Europe. In all this, we are showing how the very act, that is, the core of a vital sequence, is also regulated, defined, and thus modified by culture.

The same refers, obviously, to the third phase in a vital sequence, that of satisfaction. This, once more, can not be defined merely in terms of physiology, although physiology supplies us with the minimum definition. Satiety is undoubtedly a condition of the human organism. But an Australian aborigine who had by mistake satisfied his hunger by eating his totemic animal, an orthodox Jew who, through a mishap, had eaten pork to satiety, a Brahmin forced to eat the flesh of a cow, would one and all develop symptoms of a physiological nature, vomiting, digestive disturbances, symptoms of the illness specifically believed to be the sanction in the case of breach. The satisfaction reached by a sexual act in which the incest taboo is broken or adultery committed or the sacred vows of chastity defied produces once more an organic effect determined by cultural values. This proves that in cultural behavior we must not forget biology, but we can not rest satisfied with biological determinism alone. In regard to breathing, we might mention the very widespread belief in "evil effluvia," or dangerous atmosphere, typified in the Italian expression *mal aria,* which refers, as a rule, not to actually dangerous volatile substances, but to culturally determined categories, which produce, nevertheless, pathological results.

We see, therefore, that the bald, merely physiological consideration embodied in our table of vital sequences is a necessary point of departure, but it is not sufficient when we consider the way in which man satisfies his bodily urges under cultural conditions. In the first place, it is clear that, taking an organized human group as a whole, a culture and the people who exercise it conjointly, we have to consider each vital sequence with reference to the individual, the organized group, the traditional values, norms, and beliefs, and also the artificial environment in which most of the urges are satisfied. The concept of drive is better omitted from any analysis of human behavior, unless, that is, we understand that we have to use it differently from the animal psychologists or physiologists. Since a conceptual differentiation is always best terminologically differentiated, we shall speak henceforth of motive, meaning by this the urge as it actually is found in operation within a given culture. We have, however, to reformulate our concept of that physiological minimum, the limits within which physiological motivations can be refashioned so that they still do not force organic degeneration or depopulation upon the members of a culture. As opposed to motive, therefore, we speak of needs. This term we shall predicate not with reference to an individual organism, but rather for the community and its culture as a whole. By need, then, I understand the system of conditions in the human organism, in the cultural setting, and in the relation of both to the natural environment, which are sufficient and necessary for the survival of group and organism. A need, therefore, is the limiting set of facts. Habits and their motivations, the learned responses and the foundations of organization, must be so arranged as to allow the basic needs to be satisfied.

The concept, however, will emerge more clearly when we discuss it directly and concretely, and construct a table of needs which only indirectly corresponds to our table of impulses.

X BASIC NEEDS AND
CULTURAL RESPONSES

THE FOLLOWING TABLE of basic needs and cultural responses has been drafted with a view to simplicity. Its wording verges on triteness. Since it is, however, only a synoptic device, we shall describe each entry more fully, thus providing a definition for each of the shorthand labels.

(A) BASIC NEEDS	(B) CULTURAL RESPONSES
1. *Metabolism*	1. *Commissariat*
2. *Reproduction*	2. *Kinship*
3. *Bodily Comforts*	3. *Shelter*
4. *Safety*	4. *Protection*
5. *Movement*	5. *Activities*
6. *Growth*	6. *Training*
7. *Health*	7. *Hygiene*

Thus, the entry *metabolism* means that the processes of food intake, digestion, the collateral secretions, the absorption of nutritive substances, and rejection of waste matter are related in several ways to environmental factors and the interaction between the organism and the outside world, an interaction culturally framed. We have, thus, condensed here the several drives which were separately stated in our previous table. The supply of solid foods, of liquids, and of oxygen is all determined by the metabolic processes, and so are the processes of excretion, in which the individual once more resorts to the environment. In this context, moreover, we do not refer so much to the drive of hunger, the impulse of air intake, or the feeling of thirst. What we are concerned with here is that, as regards the community as a whole, every organism in general requires certain conditions which guarantee the supply of physical material, the conditions in which the digestive processes can be carried out and the sanitary arrangements of the end-processes.

Similarly, when we come to *reproduction*, we are not concerned with the individual drive or impulse of sex, and its realization in some particular case. Here we are stating simply that reproduction must go on in a numerically sufficiently extensive manner to replenish the numbers of the community.

The brief statement *bodily comforts* refers to the range of temperature, percentage of humidity, and absence of noxious matters in contact with the body, which allow such physiological processes as circulation, digestion, internal secretions, and metabolism to continue in the purely physical sense. Probably the range of temperature is the most significant element, since exposure to wind and weather, to rain, snow, or continuous dampness acts to a large extent through elements of temperature upon an organism.

Safety refers to the prevention of bodily injuries by mechanical accident, attack from animals or other human beings. Here it is clear that, in terms of drive, we were interested, in our previous discussion, in approximate individual types of behavior reaction to danger or to pain. Here we are putting on record that under conditions where most organisms are not protected from bodily injury the culture and its group will not survive.

The entry *movement* predicates here that activity is as necessary to the organism as it is indispensable to culture. The difference between our previous treatment of muscular and nervous impulse and the definition of the need, as it here appears, is clear. Here we are concerned with the general conditions under which a group of people live and coöperate, and under which most members at any time, and all members at some time, have to obtain some scope for exercise and initiative. The entry *growth,* which was discussed in our list of impulses, but could not be placed there, has here a legitimate position. It declares that since human beings are dependent in infancy, since maturation is a slow and gradual process, and since old age, in man more than any other animal species, leaves the individual defenceless, the facts of growing up, maturity, and decay impose certain general but very definite conditions on culture. In other words, no group could survive nor its culture endure if the infant, immediately after birth, were left to its own devices, as is the case in many animal species.

Finally, we have added here *health* as a general biological need. Whether this entry can be maintained, however, is doubtful. Obviously *health* refers to all the other entries, with the exclusion, perhaps, of the second, and even there the protection of reproductive processes from possible external dangers is part of an hygienic procedure. Indeed, if we defined health in general and positive terms, it would amount to the maintenance of the organism in normal conditions as regards its fitness for the indispensable output of energy. The only justification for making a separate entry would refer to health insofar as it is impaired and has to be regained. Since all our entries are positive, "sickness" would not be appropriate, since sickness is not a need biologically determined by its obverse. Our entry, if it reads "relief or removal of sickness or of pathological conditions," is probably justified, insofar as this imposes certain limiting conditions on human societies, and elicits certain organized responses.

Indeed, our whole two-fold list has to be read with

each pair of horizontal entries regarded as linked up inseparably. The real understanding of our concept of need
implies its direct correlation with the response which it
receives from culture. When we consider any culture
which is not on the point of breaking down or completely
disrupted, but which is a normal going concern, we find
that need and response are directly related and tuned up
to each other. The needs for food, drink, and oxygen are
never isolated, impelling forces which send the individual
organism or a group as a whole into a blind search for
food or water or oxygen, nor do people carry about
their needs for bodily comfort, for movement, or for
safety. Human beings under their conditions of culture
wake up with their morning appetite ready, and also with
a breakfast waiting for them or else ready to be prepared.
Both appetite and its satisfaction occur simultaneously as
a matter of routine. Except for accidents, the organism
maintains the necessary range of temperature from clothing, by which it is protected, the heated room or fire
burning in the shelter, or else from the necessary movement in walking, running, or economic activity. It is clear
that the organism becomes adjusted, so that within the
domain of each need specific habits are developed; and,
in the organization of cultural responses, these routine
habits are met by an organized routine of satisfactions.

This is the point in which the study of human behavior
takes a definite departure from mere biological determinism. We have made this clear already in pointing out that
within each vital sequence the impulse is refashioned or
co-determined by cultural influences. As anthropologists,
we are primarily interested in the manner in which, under
the primary organic drive, the conditioned responses of
specific taste and appetite, attraction of sex, means of
enjoyment in bodily comfort, are developed.

We are also interested in the way in which the various cultural responses are constructed. Here we shall see that these responses are by no means simple. In order to provide the constant flow of nutritive goods, articles, dress, building materials, structures, weapons, and tools, human cultures have not merely to produce artifacts, but have also to develop techniques, that is, regulated bodily movements, values, and forms of social organization. It will be best, probably, to discuss, one after the other, the various cultural responses listed in the second column, and see what they look like in details of organization and cultural structure.

1. *Commissariat.* Starting here with the direct satisfaction of the nutritive need, we would find that human beings eat and drink not by direct resort to nature, nor yet in isolation, nor yet in terms of mere anatomical or physiological performance. Were we to turn to the lowest primitives, to an Australian aboriginal tribe, to a small group of Firelanders, or to a highly sophisticated American or European community, we would come upon facts of commensalism. People often eat together on a common mat or a piece of ground reserved for that purpose, round a fireplace, round a table, or at a bar. In all this we would find that the food had already been prepared, that is, selected, cooked, roasted, and seasoned. Some physical apparatus for eating is used, table manners observed, and the social conditions of the act carefully defined. It would be possible, indeed, to show that in every human society and as regards any individual in any society the act of eating happens within a definite institution: it may be the household, a commercial eating establishment, or a hostel. It always is a fixed place, with an organization for the supply of food or its preparation, and for the opportunities of consuming it. At times the kitchen is run sepa-

rately, even in primitive communities, as when the food is cooked at home, and sent for consumption to the men's house or women's club. At times the place where food is stored is a commercial or communal establishment. But even the transferring of food already produced to the final consumer is invariably done by a series of more or less complicated organized systems of activities, that is, institutions. In our own culture, the cooking may take place thousands of miles away, as when salmon is cooked and tinned in Alaska, or lobster in South Africa, or crab in Japan, and then transported through several links in the vast commercial sequence to the consumer, who can open the can on a picnic and eat the contents even if alone. Yet this act is definitely linked up with and made possible by the very complicated chain of industrial food-preparing and food-distributing enterprises.

It is less difficult to show that production of food and its distribution are organized behavior systems, and that they form part of the tribal or national commissariat. Very often the tribe or the state enters into this, insofar as large-scale enterprise is controlled, taxed, and occasionally even organized. There are, on the one hand, cultural conditions in which production, distribution, preparation, and consumption of food are carried out within the same institution, that is, the household. This is the case even in highly advanced cultures, when an outlying agricultural farm has to rely primarily on its own production of most necessities, at least as regards food. Remarkably enough, it is less true of most primitive agricultural communities, where mutual support and exchange of services and goods are often necessary, just because of the somewhat primitive techniques used.

We see already that the cultural response to the particular need or needs imposed by metabolism consists of a set of institutions. Few of the institutions here enumerated are exclusively concerned with nutrition alone. At the same time, the very constitution of the family and of the household makes it indispensable for this group to be the predominant setting for the processes of consumption, and as a rule, also of preparation of food. If we reflect upon these facts it is clear that under conditions where nutrition depends upon the effective working of a whole chain of preparatory activities and linked institutions, every factor which would disturb the chain at any place would also affect the nutritive satisfactions. Thus, all those conditions upon which the smooth working of the chain depends become as necessary, indeed as indispensable to the biological performance as the placing of food into the individual's mouth, mastication, salivation, swallowing, and digestion.

In a community where the density of the population has reached a point for which a very complex and highly organized commissariat is indispensable, all the factors which determine the effective working of this commissariat are equally important to the end effect. In a primitive tribe leading a hand-to-mouth existence, the complexity is less but the stringency quite as great, if not greater, for here there is no surplus, there is no relying on substitute help, and the cultural margin must work consistently, and persistently, that is, with the full determinism of its constituent factors. We see here how the very efficiency of cultural response, the very fact that it provides human beings with a wider range of foods, with food which, through cooking and other preparations, is more adaptable and more digestible—how all this demands its price in imposing new limitations and requirements on human behavior. The methods of production, whether simple or complex, demand agricultural implements, weapons for hunting, nets, weirs, and traps for fishing. Methods of preserving or storing food and of cooking obviously also require supplementary apparatus. In short, the whole series of processes designated here as commissariat puts on the list of derived but indispensable necessities an extensive inventory of physical utensils, devices, or machines. These in turn have to be renewed to the extent that they deteriorate or are used up. We can see that one of the inevitable consequences already to be inferred from the working of the organized commissariat is that it imposes a by-play of constant productive activities, both in the preservation of food and in the production of all the implements for the primary food-producing, food-providing activities.

Over and above this, since, as we have seen, nutrition happens in and through organized groups and organization, we have here another element, that of minimum rules of behavior and sanctions for order and of tribal law and custom, which has to be established and maintained to keep the whole chain of activities running smoothly. Each partial activity in the food-providing process, from the planting of seed, the catching of the quarry, right up to biting, chewing, and swallowing, is normed and regulated. Rules of behavior referring to technology in every partial activity, rules of law defining ownership in terms of contribution, and rules regarding the rhythm of appetite, apportionment of the prepared product, and the manners of consuming food, are again as indispensable to the system as are its material functions. Indeed, the two can not be separated from each other. An object, whether a cooking pot or a digging stick, a plate or a fireplace, has to be skillfully, lawfully, and reverently manipulated, since it is very often effective not merely by technology, but also by customary or ethical regulation. Another dimension, that of the establishment of prescribed behavior, thus comes into being as a derived need or cultural imperative, which must be kept in working order within each human group.

If we were to look for the ways in which regulated behavior comes into being and is sustained, we would find them in two processes, that of training and that of authority. Thus educational systems, the gradual imparting of skills, knowledge, custom and ethical principles, must exist in every culture. Without training, the working personnel of any and every institution could not be continuously renewed as older members fall out through death, age, or inability to coöperate, and have to be replaced by new organisms. The enforcement of rules, as well as the moving power behind all training, implies the element of coercion or authority. We can define this as the political dimension, which is never absent from any culture, and constitutes the fourth instrumental imperative, besides education, economics, and juridical mechanisms.

2. *Kinship.* Under this brief label we have condensed the procreative processes which, in human cultures, correspond to the brief pairing and reproductive phases in animal life. The main distinction between human and animal mating is, no doubt, biologically determined, as is the need of reproduction itself. The human infant needs parental protection for a much longer period than does the young of even the highest anthropoid apes. Hence, no culture could endure in which the act of reproduction, that is, mating, pregnancy, and childbirth, was not linked up with the fact of legally-founded parenthood, that is, a relationship in which the father and the mother have to look after the children for a long period, and, in turn, derive certain benefits for the care and trouble taken.

We have already discussed the various institutions corresponding to the long-drawn-out reproductive cycle. In most communities courtship itself is an institution, or else it is carried on as a part of another institution. In some primitive cultures we have such material arrangements as the unmarried men's club or house, the marriageable girls' living quarters, both with definite rules of communal living, with internal authority, or supervision, with special arrangements for sleeping, eating, and joint activities. In conjunction with this, there are occasions for individual meeting and dalliance between boys and girls. There are very clearly defined codes of behavior, and limits to liberties with regard to one pair or the relation between various partners. All such regulated behavior is definitely oriented towards a potential contract of marriage between two partners. Young people become acquainted with each other, have opportunities for gauging mutual ability to work, qualities of companionship, very often physiological characteristics as regards direct conjugation. In other cultures, courtship is carried out in the home of the girl or by special arrangements between the families. It is always organized into a specific institutional system, or as an interplay between already organized households, village arrangements, and seasons of dancing, festivities, or carnivals. In all this, we would find that an intelligent and competent description by an ethnographic observer would have to include an account of the material apparatus involved, the personnel in terms of status, organization, and wealth, the rules which control the activities, and the sanctions, that is, the authority which watches over the ethical and legal principles involved and also supports the etiquette of the performance.

The contract of marriage establishes an independent household, even when the new-married couple continue to live either in the girl's parents' home or with the family of the bridegroom. Their incorporation is clearly determined as regards space, activities, rules of behavior, and submission to authority. The privacy of conjugal life has always to be materially determined. Economic coöperation may surround the newly-established hearth and home, or it may be a substantial addition to one already established. In either case, the new small group is already the core of a new institution which has to be defined by the analysis of its physical setting, the rules embodied, the relation of the newly wedded to their respective families, and their legal, economic, and social status.

Obviously the new group, even before reproduction sets in, does not remain isolated, but stands in close relationship to the two parental homes, the local community, and even a wider tribal setting. The act of wedding, as well as the status of *connubium*, are matters of public interest, because they are a legal relationship. Even this most private phase of human existence becomes immediately a matter of social interests, insofar as most of its ways are traditionally defined in terms of customary law, personnel, ethics, and religious belief.

With the process of pregnancy and childbirth, marriage is transformed into parenthood. Here, once more, the process never remains purely physiological or private. Invariably a set of rules of behavior becomes incumbent on the pregnant woman and her husband. They usually are sanctioned by beliefs referring to the welfare of the forthcoming new organism, and since the whole community, especially the kinsmen and kinswomen, are interested in the fact of birth and in the addition to their numbers, the proleptic customs and ethics of pregnancy and early stages of parenthood are a matter of public concern.

We need not enter here into the extension of parenthood into derived bonds of kinship. It is clear that these are, on the one hand, results and consequences of the fundamental biological processes of reproduction. On the other hand, they are highly re-defined in terms of the legal system of descent, ancestor mythology, and legal concepts defining such units as the extended family, the kindred group, and the clan. Traditional re-interpretations of the very processes of physiological pregnancy and childbirth; re-interpretations which draw into the physiological factors influences coming from the world of the dead, from the environment, and from the interaction of other members of the community, transform the innate forces of maternity and fatherhood into highly removed, yet through training and learning, powerful bonds of social solidarity.

In all this it is obvious that the student of culture has once more to relate the physiology and psychology of reproduction to the physical setting in which culture places and confines the course of the process. The economic basis of courtship, mating, marriage, and parenthood is indispensable for the understanding of how physiology is transformed into knowledge, belief, and social bonds. Here, obviously, under the term *economic*, we have subsumed material arrangements, techniques, processes of production, joint hold and use of wealth, facts of consumption, and elements of value. The legal rules which define large sections of the economic processes but which also dictate forms of marriage, establish the sanctions of its validity, and declare the consequences of marriage in terms of descent, have to be precisely stated. In other words, we have to be aware how the rules of customary law, courtship, marriage, descent, and extended kinship are formulated, where they run smoothly or else give rise to difficulties and complications, and the manner in which they are sanctioned through coercion or belief. That the educational element enters very deeply into the parental relationship is so obvious that no extensive arguments are needed. In short, we can say, first and foremost, that the understanding of cultural responses to the need of propagation requires a consecutive, substantial analysis of its component institutions, from courtship to the most extensive kinship differentiation of the tribe. Since all these institutions are related, no ethnographic account of them, nor yet a theoretical treatment, can be satisfactory, unless the relationship, as well as each partial institution, is fully described and analyzed. We have shown that over and above the determinants of biology—in its minimum form the vital sequence of attraction, conjugation, impregnation, gestation, and childbirth—there enter, with the full force of ineluctable cultural determinism, the elements of economic, educational, legal, and political determinism. We have also indicated, albeit tentatively, that elements of tribal tradition, as regards knowledge, belief, and moral value, appear also as cogent factors, without which the system of kinship can not be understood, because such psychological or symbolic factors play a vital part in the constitution of the system.

3. *Shelter* as response to *bodily comforts*. Were we to think of the simple physical factors used by human beings to insure the optimum of bodily temperature, as in the use of clothing, fire, and enclosed spaces; or of bodily cleanliness, as in ablution with water, remote and secluded places for excretion, or the more complex chemical solvents, such as alkaline substances—we would probably be somewhat at a loss to find, under this heading, new institutionalized responses. Yet here, once more, we only need to remember that human beings do not look for shelter in a haphazard manner when a squall of wind carries a shower, when the temperature suddenly rises or falls, or when a

man, drenched by immersion in water or by rain, wishes to warm himself in a cave or a house. Nor do primitive or sophisticated human beings snatch up a fur, a skin, a fabric, when they need protection. All such physical commodities are used as a routine part of organized life. Shelter, warmth, arrangements for cleanliness, may be found within the household. Clothing, however elementary or complex, is produced, under closest household economy, within the domestic group; or in a community where a division of functions exists, by organized workshops or factories. Sanitary institutions may be private or public, and thus part of the household or an integral public element within a municipality, local group, or a horde. Everywhere we would find that we have to inquire into organized production, into the incorporation of certain material objects within an institution, into the rules of decency, cleanliness, ownership, and magico-religious taboos; into the type of training carried on by an organized group, in which such habits are implanted and maintained. And as everywhere else, we would find here that, since we deal with behavior in which social and traditional regulation aims at curbing, or at least at modifying and standardizing of natural impulse, and laws of property impose a limitation of use, some authority must be there to impose sanctions, punish breach, and thus maintain order and the smooth running of organized behavior.

4. *Protection.* The organization of defence against natural danger or cataclysm, against animal attack or human violence, obviously involves such institutions as the household, the municipality, the clan, the age-grade, and the tribe. Here two important considerations enter. Protection very often consists in the exercise of foresight and in planning. The construction of houses on piles, planted either on solid ground or in a shallow lagoon or

in a lake; the erection of palisades or walls; the very selection of the site so as to avoid the danger of a tidal wave, a volcanic eruption, or an earthquake—all such anticipatory protection would have to be correlated with the biological need of safety, and its cultural responses of protection. Here, once more, the economic factor in the organized, technically planned, and coöperatively executed principles of selection, construction, and maintenance enters clearly and definitely. Rules of technique, their translation into laws of behavior, of property, of authority, are clear. Training means that the growing generation has to be prepared, enlightened, and advised.

As regards protection against human enemies or dangerous animals, we have, at this point, the main motive which makes man, however primitive or developed, organize his armed forces of resistance and aggression. Under certain types of habitat and under very primitive conditions of life, where the density of population in relation to territory is very low, the need for armed organization is insignificant. It is confined, as a rule, to the fact that each male has some elementary instruments for warding off armed attack and for carrying it out. From all the ethnographic evidence at hand, it seems probable that the political element, that is, the means of enforcing one's point of view by the argument of direct bodily violence, is very little integrated and not at all extensive. In our terminology we would say that political authority resides primarily in such small institutions as the family, clan, or municipal group. The development of individual military institutions occurs probably as a very late evolution. What we are interested in here, however, is, first and foremost, that the organization of protection, whether in the form of resistance to natural forces and animals or human beings, is invariably institutionalized. In other words, we would have, in each case, to study the material setting—the equipment in artifacts, the system of rules, the organization of the personnel, and the relation of such organized groups to the biological need of self-preservation and to the economic, legal, educational, and political techniques employed. Here also the reliance on help, as well as the fear of danger, is usually re-interpreted by primitive and developed tradition, partly in terms of well-established scientific knowledge, partly in terms of belief, mythological and personal, or the sense of responsibility to supernatural commands and persons.

5. *Activities.* The human organism, normal and rested, needs movement. This is a very general imperative imposed by human nature upon civilization. The satisfaction of this need is, on the one hand, essentially determined by the fact that without muscular action and a definite orientation of the nervous system, man achieves nothing. Thus, the systems of bodily activities connected with economics, political organization, exploration of the environment, contact with other communities, are one and all related to individual muscular tensions and their surplus of nervous energy. On the other hand, they are all instrumental, that is, directed towards the satisfaction of other needs. Hence, they are organized, that is, they can be described, submitted to theoretical analysis, and compared only in terms of institutions. There is, however, a wide field here for combined biological, psychological, and cultural research into special established and organized activities, such as sports, games, dances, and festivities, where a regulated, established muscular and nervous activity becomes an end in itself. We have a body of research on the subject of play and recreation, in which some of the answers to these problems have already been advanced. A perusal of the well-known books by K. Groos and the

recent interesting volume by J. Huizinga shows, as far as I can see, that here also both our main principles, that is, an institutional setting of the problem, and secondly, an analysis of play and recreative activities in terms of their educational value and their function as preparation for economic skills, and also as related to certain physiological needs which we can term artistic, relate most of the work done to our main methodological requirements.

6. *Growth.* This entry indicates that a full cultural analysis in descriptive terms, or as part of a scientific theory, must project the whole gamut of cultural processes and products onto the life history of a representative individual—or, where there is a substantial difference as regards class, caste, or status, of a number of representative individuals. Most ethnographic records give a description of various phases such as infancy, childhood, maturity, and old age. The scientific point of view, however, would insist on dealing not so much with the generalized description of each phase, but rather with the manner in which the individual is gradually trained in skills, taught to use language and other symbolic devices of his culture, made to enter the ever-widening set of institutions of which he will become a full member when he reaches full maturity and assumes his share of tribal citizenship. The whole set of problems now elaborated under the heading of culture and personality obviously enters here.

Once more we insist that here we would have the most appropriate place for the treatment of all the educational and socializing systems of the tribe, and that the study of this problem would consist largely in a detailed and comprehensive appreciation of how the growing organism is gradually absorbed into one institution after the other. This would demonstrate the fact that most of the training is differentiated according to the institution. The foundations of all symbolic knowledge, the first elements, that is, of the scientific outlook, the appreciation of custom, authority, and ethics, are received within the family. Later on, the growing child enters the group of his playmates, where, once more, he is drilled towards conformity, obedience to custom and etiquette. Specific economic apprenticeship is given to him when he becomes a coöperative member of an economic team or of a military society, a group, or an age-grade. There is no doubt that the most dramatic phases of education are sometimes incorporated into initiation ceremonies. But the gradual, ever-growing, increasingly complex apprenticeship to tribal life is a continuous process, a knowledge of which gives us the clue to many a fundamental problem of human organization, technology, knowledge, and belief.

7. *Hygiene.* As regards this problem, we would first have to link it up with all that refers to organic welfare in the other entries. Thus sanitary arrangements, previously discussed, might be analyzed here from the point of view of native beliefs as to health and magical dangers. Besides such considerations, the ethnographer would have to register here the minimum of elementary common sense, rules about exposure, extreme fatigue, the avoidance of dangers, of accidents, as well as the limited but never absent range of household remedies. In most primitive cultures, however, this aspect of cultural response is primarily dominated by beliefs in witchcraft or sorcery, that is, the magical power of certain people or agencies to inflict bodily harm upon man. We shall discuss this more fully when we come to analyze the formation of such beliefs.

Looking back at the argument contained in this section, we find first that in comparing the two entries *biological needs* and *cultural responses,* we have not been constructing any hypothesis or advancing any fictitious or even constructive theoretical arguments. We merely summed up two sets of empirical fact; we placed them in juxtaposition; and we drew a few inferences, strictly inductive and empirical again. Biological needs are, in our analysis, clear facts of natural science. We defined them with direct reference to our concept of vital sequence, that is, of a minimum of physiological determinism and performance which has to be incorporated into every culture. The incorporation of the vital sequences into the activities of all individuals, as regards most of them, and as regards reproduction of a sufficient number to keep up the normal density of population, we defined as a biological need. Biological needs can obviously be predicated in terms of physiological and ecological facts only with reference to the community as a whole and to its culture. The statement that under any system of organization and cultural equipment the biological needs have to be satisfied means that in whatever environment, arctic or tropic, desert or steppe, small island or impenetrable jungle, human beings must be protected against such physical influences as would damage permanently the human body or increasingly sap its energies; that they must be kept within a definite range of temperature; that they must have air for breathing, food for nutrition, and water to quench thirst.

In our listing and our definition of cultural responses, we have again merely summed up the evidence of ethnography in terms of observed fact. The inductive survey of cultural behavior, from the most primitive to the most highly developed, shows us that all physiological processes are standardized, that is, molded with reference to certain ends; that they are associated with an artificial equipment related directly to human anatomical physiology and the goals of human activities. We have also seen that all such responses are carried out collectively, and follow a number of traditional rules.

In examining the character of the cultural responses to each biological need, we discovered that we do not find a simple or exclusively oriented cultural apparatus, aiming at the satisfaction of hunger or related exclusively to reproduction or safety or the maintenance of health. What actually occurs is a chained series of institutions, related to each other within each chain but also, one and all, appearing virtually under every single heading. We are satisfied by being once more led to the conclusion that our concept of institution provides us with the legitimate unit of concrete analysis. Yet the problem of this multiple appearance of institutions and the absence of point-for-point correlation between biological need and institutionalized response will require a few words of further discussion.

We have, however, come upon a different concept in the course of our analysis. We found that human activities can also be classified according to the type, subject matter, and specific end. We found everywhere a strand of economic interest and organization, of educational influence, of customary or legal stringency, and of political authority. These four instrumental needs appeared as the four main types of activity distributed under family, age-grade, clan, coöperative team, or secret society.

It would not be difficult, however, to show that the two types of analyses, functional and institutional, are intimately related. Harking back to our discussion and diagrammatic representation of institutional structure, we see that besides charter, activities and function, there appear three main, concrete and tangible positions on our diagram: personnel, norms, and material apparatus. If we were right in our analysis, then obviously the upkeep, as well as the running of the material apparatus, the rules of ownership, and the techniques of production and handling, must be a collateral concomitant of all such systems of organized activities. Equally clear it is that personnel must be as much renewed and replaced as the body of implements. Hence, training in forms of physiological guidance, general instruction, or apprenticeship is a process implied by the very structure of an institution. The concept of norms implies also codification, as well as coercive factors that induce people to keep to the norms and prevent deviation. The essential concept of organization and of sanction is that of authority, as well as differentiation in services and prerogatives. Hence, political structure is also a fact which could be deduced from the analysis of our diagram.

As regards charter and function, we have not yet the necessary elements to build up this concept. Obviously charter, above all, is a piece of customary law, backed up by retrospective mythological elements in tradition. We have described charter as the definition by the group of the value, purpose, and importance of the institution into which they are organized. Hence, the formulation of the charter, as well as the codification of norms, implies a full understanding of the rôle of symbolism in culture, a point to which we will soon have to turn. As regards function, we have defined it as the satisfaction of needs. So far we have only fully analyzed the biological or basic needs, and indicated the inevitability of the derived, secondary or instrumental imperatives or cultural needs. It is clear, however, that this concept refers rather to the type of scientific analysis, the other type to human behavior, especially when we apply it to an institution as a whole.

This brings us to the question previously indicated, that is, the fact that no institution can be functionally related to one basic need, nor yet as a rule to a simple, cultural need. This really need not trouble us if we look closer at the facts. Culture is not and can not be a replica in terms of specific responses to specific biological needs. The very fact that cultural response contains a number of additional instrumentalities would be sufficient to show that the production of certain comprehensive instrumentalities and their maintenance would be best suited to the integral satisfaction of a series of needs.

This is most clearly exemplified when we consider the family. Primarily we would always relate it to the reproductive need of the community. Yet even by the simple biological consideration that the human infant is completely dependent on its primary social milieu, and that this dependence lasts for a long time, we would reach the conclusion that the natural bisexual group of man and woman who organize for conjugation and reproduction will also have to organize for protracted care and guidance of offspring. Since they have to carry on these biological or partly biological activities obviously in close contact and within the same spatial enclosure, the bodily needs of safety, comfort, and movement will be satisfied by the same physical apparatus and system of habits and rules that establish the environmental basis for reproduction. Thus the family will be always integrated on reproduction, and through the principle of propinquity, a whole range of needs, nutritive and connected with health, cleanliness, and bodily comforts, will be conjointly satisfied within the domestic organization. Hence we will find within each household an economic system of activities, a distribution of authority, while the process of training the young organism is but another side of the process of satisfying the infant's primary needs, protecting it, and guiding its early physiological stages. It is equally clear that a group of neighbors organized into a municipality will be conjointly interested in the legal aspect of reproduction, especially as regards courtship and the maintenance of such moral rules as magically sanctioned abstinences, as against incest and adultery.

In many ways also, the commissariat can never be regarded, even in the most primitive tribes, as a purely domestic affair, but involves also the municipality, and, at times, wider groups. It would be easy to show that any such wider group like the clan or the tribe in the political sense can not have any point-to-point correlation with one need, whether this be basic or instrumental. Political organization and such of its activities as defence, aggression, or large tribal gatherings, demand of course some form of feeding, housing, and climatic protection. Hence, whether we consider the clan, the age-grade, or the military force or deliberative council of a tribe, we would have to determine the whole range of needs and imperatives which have to be satisfied in the course of a successful performance. Even if we turned to very highly crystallized institutions on the highest level of culture, that is, institutions on the occupational basis, we would find that they seldom can be defined in terms of a simple and specific function. The banking system is obviously concerned primarily with the supply of credit and the handling of investments and the capitalization of enterprise. As such, however, it is also a training institution, for apprenticeship remains in every culture an integral part of every institution. In every institution we have a minimum of specialized rules and by-laws which constitute at least its routine and its traditional character. Hence, there is a legal, that is, also a political aspect, to every banking institution. If we approach any specific need, on the other hand, we find invariably a variety of organized groups, not one of which can exclusively satisfy this need. Health, even in our community, is cared for by hospitals, doctors and nurses, which might be described as the medical profession organized on the charter of scientific medicine. Nevertheless, we have also faith healing, Christian Science practitioners, intuitive osteopaths, psychoanalysts, and fresh-air, cold-water, rawfood, or sunshine unitarians, usually ready to treat every ailment by their one specific.

Does this mean that the function of an institution can not be defined at all? By no means. It is always necessary in the integral definition of function, when we come to an organized and established system of activities, to determine their essential nature, and relate to it the other subsidiary functions. The family, for instance, is, as we have repeatedly stressed, a reproductive unit. Cultural reproduction, however, includes the training of the young, for which the economic, as well as physical basis, is provided in the organized household. We can, therefore, state that the production, the ontogenetic and cultural development of the young, and their equipment for tribal life with regular status and material outfit is the function of the domestic institution. We could rephrase it even more briefly: the family transforms the raw material of the new organisms into full citizens, tribal or national. Such a definition fits all human societies. It demands, when applied to fieldwork, an answer in terms of observed fact and provides a comparative basis for any cross-cultural survey.

The integral function of the municipality consists in the organization of a neighborhood for joint and coöperative control, exploitation, and defence of the settlement and territory. Here, obviously, our definition implies an analysis in terms of a clear definition of boundaries, a statement of land tenure, including a description of the ecological and cultural classification of lands, and of the activities referring to these lands. Hence, we would have to study the main food-producing activities, such as collect-ing, hunting, fishing, agriculture, and the breeding of domesticated animals. The definition, if explicitly ana-lyzed in terms of observable fact, would also involve the distribution of authority, the definition of municipal law insofar as it coördinates and delimits the activities of the component households. We would have also to study local mythologies and the coördination of magic, religion, rec-reational festivities, and artistic productions, with refer-ence to the local group as carrier of the tradition, as bene-ficiary of the performances, and as the corporate body whose duty it is to institute, to defray, and to organize such activities.

We see, thus, that although at first sight our definitions may appear "vague, insipid, and useless," in reality they are condensed formulae which contain extensive recipes for the organization of perspective in field-work. And this really is the hallmark of scientific definition. It must prin-cipally be a call to a scientifically schematized and oriented observation of empirical fact. It also should define briefly the largest common measure of phenomena which will be found in every area of observation. Thus, also, such defini-tions functionally conceived, hence each containing the maximum of cogency and determinism, are useful both in the comparative treatment of ethnographic facts and their discovery. The cogency of the functional approach con-sists in the fact that it does not pretend to forecast exactly how a problem posed for a culture will be solved. It states, however, that the problem, since it is derived from bio-logical necessity, environmental conditions, and the nature of cultural response, is both universal and categorical.

We could state that the function of the tribe as a po-litical unit is the organization of force for policing, defence, and aggression. Here, obviously, the word "policing" implies a minimum of judiciary functions, a tribal authority or authorities which constitute a court and a social organization for the enforcement of rules. The function of age-groups is the coördinating of physiological and anatomical characteristics as they develop in the processes of growth, and their transformation into cultural categories. The function of associations is the implementing of a specific purpose, interest, or ideal by an *ad hoc* organization in which specific instrumentalities and activities are directed to the common end. In occupational groups we see that the carrying out of skills, techniques, and such activities as education, law, and power, constitute the integral function of the group. Once more, only a somewhat superficial and uninstructed anthropologist or sociologist would see, in such definitions, formulae so general and vague that they are "useless." Their utility obviously depends on the translation into concrete problems of each general term—a translation which we have exemplified in the case of our definition of the municipality, and which every ethnologist can carry out in each of the other instances.

It probably is also clear, to the reader acquainted at the same time with cultural studies and with scientific principles, that the concept of function is primarily descriptive. We might say that in introducing this concept, we are supplying a new heuristic principle in laying stress on the absolute necessity for an additional type of research. This consists primarily in a consideration of how certain devices, forms of organization, customs, or ideas enlarge the range of human potentialities on the one hand, and impose certain restrictions on human behavior on the other. In short, functionalism is the consideration of what culture is as a determining principle, in terms of the addition which it provides to the individual and collective standard of living.

This might, perhaps, dispose of the oft-repeated criticism that the function of a cultural phenomenon always consists in showing how it functions. As a statement of fact this criticism is absolutely correct. As a methodological indictment it simply discloses the low level of epistemological intelligence among anthropologists. The functionalist, to take a simple example, would insist that in describing a fork or a spoon we also must supply the information on how they are used, how they are related to table manners, to convivialism, to the nature of cooked viands and dishes, and to the layout of such apparatus of commensalism as tables, plates, tablecloths, and napkins. When an anti-functionalist remonstrates that, after all, there are cultures where neither spoons nor forks nor knives are used, and that, therefore, function explains nothing, we simply have to point out that explanation to the scientific thinker is nothing else but the most adequate description of a complex fact. The type of criticism levelled against functionalism, to the effect that it never can prove why a specific form of drum or trumpet, of table implement or theological concept, is prevalent in a culture, derives from the prescientific craving for first causes or "true causes." These can be more readily seen in the persistent search for "origins" and "historic causes," in the nebulous realms of the undocumented, unrecorded historic past or evolutionary beginnings of a people who neither have a history nor have left any traces of their previous evolution. As a matter of fact and as we have several times insisted, history explains nothing unless it can be shown that an historical happening has had full scientific determination, and that we can demonstrate this determination on the basis of well-documented data. In ethnology or history, only too often, the hunt for the "true cause" lies in completely non-determined, because non-charted, realms of hypothesis, where speculation can roam freely, unhampered by fact.

Take our example of the fork as the instrument for the conveyance of a solid morsel from plate to mouth. It is obvious that once we define its function within the domain of observable cultures, we have *de facto* reached the maximum of evidence concerning its "first origins." This momentous act in human history—for the historian and evolutionist are usually profoundly excited over exactly such trivialities as the origins of the fork or a drum or a back-scratcher—arose under the determinism of very much the same forces which keep the instrument, its uses, and its function alive in the working cultures of today. Since its form, its function, and its general context within commensality as a cultural phenomenon can be shown to be substantially the same wherever we find it, the only intelligent hypothesis as to its origin is that the origins of the fork are the performance of the minimum tasks which this instrument can perform. Again, if we were to study its diffusion or any other historical adventures, we would have here to make the absurd assumption that a fork can be used under conditions which make its use completely inadequate, that is, non-related to any needs, individual or collective, or else we would conclude reasonably that its historical destinies can be scientifically subsumed under the formula: the fork goes where it is needed and is transformed in form and function according to new needs and new local co-determinants of culture.

The contempt for function as something essentially tautological, hence irrevelant, is to be unmasked as something like intellectual laziness when we consider some of our most complex cultural achievements. Take the airplane, the submarine, or the steam engine. Obviously, man does not need to fly, nor yet to keep company with fishes, and move about within a medium for which he is neither anatomically adjusted nor physiologically prepared. In defining, therefore, the function of any of those contrivances, we can not predicate the true course of their appearance in any terms of metaphysical necessity. In terms of scientific description and theory, however, the only thing which an intelligent student of culture can do is to show the relation of such contrivances to the state of human knowledge; to the aims, purposes, and activities which are made possible by such inventions and to the influences of these mechanisms for the extension of man's bodily powers to the structure and the working of human culture as a whole. In this the real and intelligent historian would work exactly on the lines of approach of the functionalist. He could not concentrate on "form" and neglect "function." He would have to deal with the integral phenomenon, to assess all the determining factors of its appearance, and all the relevant consequences of its permanent and systematic employment.

We are thus beginning to see the nature of the derived needs in human cultures. This concept obviously means that culture supplies man with derived potentialities, abilities, and powers. This also means that the enormous extension in the range of human action, over and above innate abilities of the naked organism, imposes on man a number of limitations. In other words, culture imposes a new type of specific determinism on human behavior.

XI THE NATURE
OF DERIVED NEEDS

WE HAVE NOW to define more precisely what are those derived needs or, as we shall continue to call them, cultural imperatives imposed on man by his own tendency to extend his safety and his comforts, to venture into the dimensions of movement, to increase his speed, to prepare engines of destruction, as well as production, to armor himself with colossal protective devices and construct equivalent means of attack. If our concept of derived need or cultural imperative is correct, certain new types of behavior are implied in all cultural responses, which are as stringent and ineluctable as every vital sequence is in its own right. In other words, we have to show that man must economically coöperate, that he must establish and maintain order; that he must educate the new and growing organism of each citizen; and that he must somehow implement the means of enforcement in all such activities. We have to show how and where these activities come in and how they combine. Finally, in order to make the processes of derivation and the hierarchy of need clear, we shall have to show how economics, knowledge, religion and mechanisms of law, educational training and artistic creativeness are directly or indirectly related to the basic, that is, physiological needs.

Let us start with the stringency and determinism of the derived imperatives of culture. Humanity as a whole, and each individual in every society, start as naked organisms, unarmed, unprotected, and unequipped. Man's anatomical endowment, compared with other animals', is somewhat limited. It lacks any natural weapons, such as claws, fangs, poison receptacles. Man's teeth are not good enough for sawing wood, breaking stone, nor are his hands useful to dig the soil or to kill his prey. Instead of that, man produces sharp and heavy weapons, capable of attaining even a distant aim. He invents and develops instruments to dig, to kill or trap the prey on the ground, in the air, and in the water. He borrows animal furs and prepares textiles from vegetable fiber. The positive factor, the advantages derived from this constant and chronic exploitation of the environment for his own benefit, are as obvious as they are immense. The price which man has to pay in terms of additional determinism of his behavior is clear, too. He has to work on time, know how to do it, and become prepared to rely on his comrades at work.

Can we say, however, that the submission to cultural rules is as absolute as the submission to biological determinism? Once we realize that dependence on the cultural apparatus, however simple or complex, becomes the *conditio sine qua non,* we see immediately that the failure in social coöperation or symbolic accuracy spells immediate destruction or long-run attrition in the plain biological sense.

Man does not, by biological determinism, need to hunt with spears or bow and arrow; use poison darts; nor defend himself by stockades, by shelters, or by armor. But the moment that such devices have been adopted, in order to enhance human adaptability to the environment, they also become necessary conditions for survival. And here we can enumerate, point for point, the factors on which human dependence becomes as great as dependence on the execution of any biologically dictated vital sequences. Imagine any situation of direct, dangerous, and culturally inevitable performance. The hunter faces an animal stronger, anatomically better equipped, with whom unarmed contest must result in disablement or death. The object which he uses, his spear, his bow and arrow, or his gun, must be technically perfect. His skill and ability to use it can not fail at the crucial moment. In a coöperative hunting expedition the weapon, as well as the fellow hunters, must be at the right place and the right moment, and must do their work. In this, symbolic communication has to be adequate if failure is to be prevented. Thus, the material equipment in its economic production and technical quality, the skills based on training, knowledge and experience, the rules of coöperation, and symbolic efficiency are one and all as indispensable under the ultimate sanction of the biological imperative of self-preservation as are any purely physiologically determined elements.

Let us briefly consider the long-run consequences of failure. Whether we look at a primitive tribe or at a highly developed nation, we see that they do not only depend for their survival on what the environment gives them to eat, to clothe themselves, to safeguard their bodily integrity and their health. To produce all objects, they must follow the techniques, regulate collective behavior, and keep alive the tradition of knowledge, law, and ethics by a system of activities which, on analysis, can be shown to be economic, legal, educational, political, scientific, magical, religious, and ethical. A permanent deterioration in material equipment, in social solidarity, in the training of the individual and the development of his abilities, would lead in the long run, not merely to the disorganization of culture, but also to starvation, large-scale disease, the deterioration of personal efficiency, hence also, obviously, to depopulation.

Since the collective and integral functioning of a culture, high or low, supplies the means for the satisfaction of biological needs, every aspect of the collective production, in the widest sense of the word, is biologically as necessary as the full and adequate carrying out of all the vital sequences. In primitive cultures the adherence to tradition, often described as conservative, slavish, or automatic, is perfectly comprehensible through the consideration that the simpler human knowledge, skills and material equipment are, the more definitely they must be maintained at an efficient working level. There are very few alternative devices, the numbers of those who carry the knowledge and the tradition are limited. Hence, adherence to what is known and what can be effectively performed has to be great.

In a highly developed culture we have a whole set of specific devices to insure this adherence to our scientific tradition, to our economic organization, and to the accuracy of our symbolic transmission of ideas and principles.

Here, if we want to test our principle of stringency and derived needs, we could well refer to the dramatic demonstration thereof in the present historical world situation. The integral world wars are not waged merely by implements of destruction. Here, obviously, the ultimate aim of this instrumental approach is also biological: the extermination of human organisms. Indirectly, however, here also the victorious army often achieves its ends by disorganizing and confusing the opponents, and thus forcing them to surrender. The integral war, however, has its concomitants in economic battles, in the contest of nerves, and in propaganda. Here we see that if in an economic war a large modern nation can impose conditions of starvation or even malnutrition, surrender will be achieved by the break-down of an instrumental apparatus of organized food-production or food import. If, through economic warfare, the supply of raw materials for industrial production can be cut off, destroyed, or labor subverted, we see once more how indirectly and through many relays, the destruction of one of the instrumental, large-scale devices will affect the biological efficiency of a large modern community. By sapping or undermining the organization, the morale, and the symbolically implemented relation between people, one organized state can, under conditions of war, defeat another. Propaganda, through fifth-column tactics, sometimes introduces what might be called a sociologically disoriented symbolism. When, in the overwhelming of Norway, treacherous orders were given to Norwegian units by German agents, these were correctly formulated symbolic orders placed in the wrong, that is, falsely apprehended, position of authority.

A fuller consideration of concrete processes in all these facts would show that war, with its battles of violence, economic attack, and propaganda, becomes effective as a means of coercion only when it finally reaches the biological level of human welfare. Killing, maiming, exposure to formidable sound and sight, act directly on body and nervous system. Such confusion as occurred in the terrified areas of the Lowlands and France, with the complete uprooting of refugees, congested roads, exposure to cold and weather, were all facts which could be described only in terms of human bodies and physical suffering and the disorder in direct human movements.

We can thus see, first and foremost, that derived needs have the same stringency as biological needs, and that this stringency is due to the fact that they are always instrumentally related to the wants of the organism. We see also how and where they come into the structure of human organized behavior. We see, finally, that even such highly derived activities as learning and research, art and religion, law and ethics, related as they are with organized performance, with technology, and with accuracy of communication, are also definitely related, although by several removes, to the necessity of human beings to survive, to retain health and a normal state of organic efficiency. In all this it is hardly necessary to emphasize that our concepts and arguments have never moved outside the empirical level of analysis indispensable for a full understanding, that is a correct, objective, and adequate description of facts.

It remains now only to tabulate our results and to define the entries clearly and briefly. The adjoining synopsis states, in the first column, the instrumental imperatives of culture so far encountered in our analysis. Also are listed briefly the cultural responses to these imperatives.

IMPERATIVES	RESPONSES
1. The cultural apparatus of implements and consumers' goods must be produced, used, maintained, and replaced by new production.	1. Economics
2. Human behavior, as regards its technical, customary, legal, or moral prescription must be codified, regulated in action and sanction.	2. Social control
3. The human material by which every institution is maintained must be renewed, formed, drilled, and provided with full knowledge of tribal tradition.	3. Education
4. Authority within each institution must be defined, equipped with powers, and endowed with means of forceful execution of its orders.	4. Political organization

There is no need for us to commence with the first set of entries. We have already shown why they must be regarded as stringent and imposing a new type of derived imperatives on human behavior. We have also shown the process of derivation, and thus linked up the instrumental determinism of cultural activities with the basic source of this determinism, that is, biological requirements.

As regards the second column, it is clear that economic activities always form part of more general institutions, such as the family, clan, municipality, political tribe, or age-grade. At times even on primitive levels, human beings organize in principle for specific institutions. A team of food gatherers, an organized hunting or fishing band, a group of people carrying on conjointly the agricultural work of the community are primarily economic institutions on a primitive level. As culture develops, specific productive, marketing, and consuming groups appear. In the highest cultures, the organization of industry, finance, banking, coöperatives, and consumers' unions need hardly be mentioned as typical predominantly economic institutions.

It is important, however, to realize that the economic system of a culture, taken as a whole, implies not merely the descriptive inventory of the various institutions for the production, exchange, and consumption of goods, but also an analysis in terms of general principles controlling the economics of a community as a whole. Economics is the study of the production, exchange, distribution, and consumption of wealth. Wealth differs profoundly along the line of evolutionary level, or environmental differentiation, and it depends on a number of legal rules or conceptions of value defined by tradition. The integral study of the whole process, starting with the factors of production, the organization of exchange and distribution, and the manner in which wealth is partly consumed, partly used as an instrument of power, deals with these general principles that control each specific economic institution within a given culture, and it is additional to the study of each specific institution. The classic economic theory has to be partly tested, partly re-framed in more elastic terms in defining such concepts as land, labor, capital, and the organization of enterprise on levels where these terms can not be borrowed from our own culture.

Nevertheless, in my opinion, the general structure of the classical theory is applicable, with modifications. Certainly the analysis of "land," that is, all the environmental resources in terms of rights of property, selective use, and appreciation in terms of mythology, magic, religion, and local patriotism, is indispensable. The organization of labor in relation to "land," but which is primarily connected with domestic differentiation of functions or with the clan system or with some form of social stratification culminating in slavery, is a descriptive problem for the field-worker, and it would supply a general theory of man's economic attitudes with valuable comparative material. The concept of capital as a body of instrumental wealth, including perhaps accumulated food, is as useful in primitive economics as in the classical theory. The organization of marketing and exchange leads obviously to the question of exchange as a mere token of good-will. A somewhat complex problem arises concerning the mechanisms and means of exchange. One of the main sources of error in many anthropological records is the loose usage of the concept of money. Indeed, the anthropologist could have rendered a great deal of service to the history of economic development and to our understanding of money if he had analyzed this concept into its elementary component parts, and studied the use of certain commodities as standards of value, as common means of exchange, and as measures of deferred payment, and provided data for the history of the gradual development and integration of money as a general medium in commercial transactions.

We do not need, however, to dwell here upon the technicalities in the methods and principles of primitive economics. The main point is that the problem of the functional response to the need of permanent renewal of the material apparatus establishes an approach and a theoretical perspective which is not completely covered by the concrete institutional analysis. Here we have a specific functional question of how culture, as an integral mechanism, is organized so as to satisfy the instrumental imperatives by a consistent and coherent system of typical responses. Such an answer would contain—or at least lead us to—a fuller definition of what we mean by economic determinism, or by the economic quota and economic motivation in a network of complex behavior carried on under multiple motivation. Personally, I would define economic in its adjectival form as this aspect of human behavior which is connected with ownership, that is, the use or right of disposal of wealth, that is, material goods specifically appropriated. It is obvious that this definition implies also the concept of economic value, that specific culturally determined drive towards exclusive appropriation of certain claims to use, to consume, and to enjoy material possession to the exclusion of others.

As regards our second entry, social control, this declares that in every community there are to be found means and ways by which the members become cognizant of their prerogatives and duties; that there are impelling reasons and mechanisms which keep each individual to the by-and-large full performance of his duty, and thus also to the adequate satisfaction of his privilege; and finally, that in case of deviation or breach, there are some means for the re-establishment of order and the satisfaction of unfulfilled claims. The absence of clearly crystallized legal institutions in some simple societies has often led the ethnographer to the ignoring of this functional problem. The way in which we have formulated it here, however, demonstrates that, to a permanent and cogent, albeit derived need, there must be given a definite and adequate response. Hence here again our approach is primarily a call for fuller, better oriented, and more effective research in the field. The main point of orientation here would be that it is necessary to study the manner in which the various rules are inculcated into the individual during his lifetime. This obviously is part of the educational problem. But here what might be called the normative or legal approach would redirect the observers' attention to the manner in which training, from its earliest phases up to full tribal initiations or apprenticeship, not merely compels general respect and obedience to tribal tradition but also reveals to the individual the consequences and penalties of deviation or breach. It would be found, probably, that very often the element of force or of coercive violence appears at the stage of training and drill, rather than punishment for the breach of custom. Parental authority is notoriously lax and soft among so-called primitives. There are, however, other agencies of coercive training which supplement or substitute domestic authority: the group of playmates, the rigid discipline of initiation camps, the severe apprenticeship which prepares a boy or a youth to take part in economic enterprise or military activities, and an organized system of sanctions in the educational or biological line of development. Here, also, the good fieldworker would have to enter more fully into the actual manner in which public opinion exercises its pressure from childhood towards maturity.

Again, at the later age when the mature individual becomes a member of an institution, most of the sanctions which compel him to play his rôle correctly are due not to the organized exercise of central authority within the group, whether this be the head of a domestic group, the leader of a clan, the headman of a municipality, or the chief of the tribelet. The most stringent, compelling forces result from the concatenation of service and counter-service, from the impelling force of an empirically founded realization that a slacker, an incompetent, or dishonest collaborator gradually falls out of the institutions, becomes ostracized or expelled. He thus gradually sinks to the position of more or less complete insignificance and ineffectuality, from which he can only lift himself by more scrupulous and adequate resumption of his duties. It is in such a detailed, concrete, and comprehensive study of the normative aspect of primitive life that we learn to understand the real nature of what is usually described as the "primitive's slavish adherence to rule, custom, and taboo." As regards education, we have merely to state here once more that there are few specific institutions, and that the processes of training, of drill, of implanting of correct attitudes and manners are inherent in the working of each institution. The most important of these, obviously, is the domestic group, but it will be found that every organized institution provides for specific apprenticeship, in which the newly incorporated member has first of all to learn the rules of trade, of social duty, of etiquette, and of ethics.

Our definition of the political aspect in human organization can be narrowed down to the use of direct force by individuals in authority over the other members of the group. Starting from observations of the occasions on which bodily violence actually occurs, of the techniques and legal limitations thereof and the reasons for which it is allowed, we would then study how it is gradually transformed into attitudes of obedience and acquiescence on the one hand, limited and justified, or else of tyranny and abuse of power on the other. Obviously here the organization of violence will be definitely related to the position of the group with regard to others with whom it lives, either on a peaceful footing or under conditions of war.

XII THE INTEGRATIVE IMPERA-
TIVES OF HUMAN CULTURE

THROUGH ALL OUR arguments we have implied that rules of conduct are known, and that they are transmitted by tradition. In our concept of charter, which is crucial to our institutional analysis, we spoke about codes of constitutional rules, about mythological ideas, and about values that provide and integrate the behavior of an organized group.

All this still remains somewhat in the air so long as we can not define, in terms of our analysis of culture, such phenomena as language, oral or written tradition, the nature of some dominant dogmatic concepts, and the way in which subtle moral rules are incorporated into human behavior. Everyone knows that all this is based primarily on verbal instruction or linguistic texts, that is, on the whole realm of symbolism. I shall try to show here that symbolism is an essential ingredient of all organized behavior; that it must have come into being with the earliest appearance of cultural behavior; and that it is a subject matter which can be submitted to observation and theoretical analysis in terms of objective fact, to the same extent to which we can observe material artifacts, collective movements of groups, or define the form of a custom. The central thesis here maintained is that symbolism, in its essential nature, is the modification of the original organism which allows the transformation of a physiological drive into a cultural value.

In discussing this problem with reference to very simple cultures, and in terms of "origins," we shall once more use the procedure of examining cultural phenomena, complex and simple alike, and trace the permanent and inevitable implications that control every phase of cultural behavior. Thus, the concept of origins means for us simply the minimum conditions necessary and sufficient for the distinction of pre-cultural as against cultural activity. Were we to consider some of the most essential adaptations between man and his environment, such as shelter, warmth, clothing, food, or weapons, we would find that they imply modifications both in the organism and the environment. This general principle obviously runs from the highest to the lowest level, and it is a principle which we have fully established already. Let us, for a moment, face the imaginary situation of the birth of culture. I maintain that from our knowledge of modern stimulus-response psychology, of animal training, of infant psychology, as well as ethnographic evidence, we can reconstruct not the exact moment and form in which culture was born, but certainly the conditions necessary and sufficient for the transformation of animal into cultural behavior. We know that not only apes, such as have been used in the studies of Yerkes, Köhler, and Zuckermann, but also all performing animals, from elephants to fleas, and certainly the rats, guinea pigs and dogs used by Pavlov, Bechterev, and Hull, can develop very complex habits. The elasticity and range of their learning is limited, but it goes very far towards the demonstration that animals can make inventions, be taught to use devices, to handle complex apparatus, to appreciate value tokens, and thus satisfy their primary needs by what is, in fact, a fairly complex cultural apparatus.

From this material we can already state a number of general principles. Since the problem of the student of culture differs profoundly from that of the psychologist, our statement will not completely conform with the general theory of stimulus-response psychology, which is now in the process of gradual elaboration. The stimulus-response psychologist is primarily interested in the full analysis of the process of learning. To the student of culture the value of this research lies mainly in the total situation and all the agencies of learning. Thus, for instance, the psychologist is especially interested in his own performance and rôle, and he very often takes the general setting of the experiment for granted. Not so the student of culture.

The way in which we anthropologists can project the experimental situation of the animal onto the beginnings of culture is by isolating the main factors which must be present if the habit is to be formed. The prehuman ancestors of our species were obviously able to discover certain devices to achieve individual habits and to use in such an achievement certain instrumentalities. The essential set of determining factors indispensable for each such achievement were, first, the existence of a strong organic drive, such as provided by the nutritive need, or the reproductive, or the complex set which we have labelled as bodily comforts. The drive would appear as hunger, sexual urge, pain, escape from imminent danger, and avoidance of noxious circumstances and conditions. The equivalent of the conditioning apparatus must have been the absence of direct satisfaction, together with certain instrumentalities which allowed the goal to be reached. The detailed description by Köhler of how his chimpanzees in captivity were able to obtain food, companionship, and other desirable ends by a clearly instrumental appreciation indicates that, under conditions of nature, higher apes or pre-cultural human ancestors would also be able to select objects, devise techniques, and thus enter upon instrumental and yet pre-cultural action. Such habits may have been individually retained under the mechanisms of reinforcement, that is, of the satisfaction following the instrumental performance. In terms of our cultural analysis, reinforcement is nothing else but the direct connection within the individual organism between the drive, the instrumentality, and its satisfaction.

We can thus imagine that tools, weapons, shelters, and effective methods of courtship could be discovered, invented, and transformed into individual habits. Each such individual performance or achievement would imply for the pre-cultural individual, as it does for the animal, the appreciation of a material object as an implement, of its use as a reinforced habit, and of the integral connection between drive, habit, and satisfaction. In other words, artifact, norm, and value are already present in animal learning, and probably were present in the pre-cultural behavior of anthropoid apes and of the notorious "missing link." Yet as long as such habits had to be individually improvised and could not be made the basis of learned behavior for all the individuals of a community, we can not speak yet about culture. The transition between the pre-cultural achievements and abilities of animals, and the stable, permanent organization of activities which we call culture, is marked by the distinction between habit and custom. With this we also have to register the distinction between the improvised instruments and the body of traditionally handed-over artifacts; between invented and re-invented forms of habit and traditionally defined rules; between sporadic and individual achievement and permanently organized group behavior.

All this hinges upon the ability of a group to incorporate the principles of individual achievement into a tradition which can be communicated to other members of the group and also, which is even more important, transmitted from one generation to the other. This means that through some means or other every member of the community could become aware of the form, the material, the technique, and the value of a technical device, of a method of obtaining food, safety, or a mate. Before we inquire as to the exact means by which all those elements of knowledge, organization, and appreciation could be standardized, we have to state that the process implies definitely the existence of a group and also the existence of a permanent relation between its members. Thus, any discussion of symbolism without its sociological context is futile, like any assumption that culture could originate without the simultaneous appearance of artifacts, techniques, organization, and symbolism. In other words, what we can state already is that the origins of culture can be defined as the concurrent integration of several lines of development: the ability to recognize instrumental objects, the appreciation of their technical efficiency, and their value, that is, their place in the purposive sequence, the formation of social bonds, and the appearance of symbolism.

XIII   THE INSTRUMENTALLY
IMPLEMENTED VITAL
SEQUENCE

We have stated our functional analysis of culture from the concept of the vital sequence, that is, the relation between drive, its physiological consummation, and the state of organic satisfaction. It will be useful to incorporate our new analysis into the previous diagram.

Diagram of Instrumental Sequence

DRIVE (1) → INSTRUMENTAL PERFORMANCE ⎰ 1. Object
2. Technique
3. Coöperation or tradition
4. Context of situation ⎱

↓

DRIVE (2) → CONSUMMATION GOAL-RESPONSE ————————→ SATISFACTION

We have here diagrammatically represented the cultural equivalent of the vital sequence. This represents the phase of human behavior which is typical of any and every activity connected with the satisfaction of needs. The difference between this and our previous diagram consists, first, in the insertion of the instrumental performance, which becomes an essential link in the pragmatic series. We have also duplicated the entry *drive* and distinguished it by numerical indices. This represents the fact that the initial drive which sets in for all animal learning, in animal behavior after the habit has been acquired and in all human cultural activities, leads not directly to the goal but to the instrumentalities through which the goal can be reached. We do not need to elaborate this, since a great deal of our previous argument bears on this fact. Drive (2) represents the fact that after the instrumental phase had been adequately accomplished, the immediate drive of nutritive or sexual appetite, of removal of pain or noxious bodily conditions, leads directly towards the physiological performance, whether this be positive or negative, the satisfaction of pleasure or the removal of pain. Yet it is clear that the reinforcement also refers to the situation where Drive (2) can be effectively satisfied. Since the instrumental performance is an integral part of the series, the reinforcement, or as the psychologists like to call it, the secondary reinforcement, becomes attached to the instrumental performance as a whole, and to all its component parts: the artifact, the technique, the rules of coöperation, and the context of situation. All these elements become pervaded with the physiologically determined, pleasurable tone. They become, in a derived or secondary manner, objects of desire; they become imbued with a pleasurable tone characteristic of successful execution of a vital sequence. The organism, in short, reacts to the instrumental elements with the same or at least similar appetitive force as it does to objects which reward it directly by physiological pleasure. We can define this strong and inevitable attachment of the organism to certain objectives, norms, or persons who are instrumental to the satisfaction of the organism's need, by the term *value,* in the widest sense of the word. It is interesting to note that, to a large extent, we have already foreshadowed the main elements of the symbolic in culture. For symbolism, in the crudest way in which it is often defined, means that something stands for something else; or that the sign or symbol contains in it an idea, an emotion, or some other portion of the introspectively known substance of "consciousness."

We shall see that all such definitions are metaphysically tainted, and that, in reality, symbolism is founded not in a mysterious relation between the sign and the contents of the human mind, but between an object, a gesture, and an action and its influence upon the receptive organism. And here we have seen how, through the instrumental extension of the vital sequence, an object, a technical gesture, the presence of another person and his behavior, become calls or inducements to the performance of an instrumental activity. Our diagram illustrates that the necessary implement or technique or coöperative device is gradually transformed into a pragmatic signal in the same way that food is a pragmatic symbol to a hungry organism or a female to a male animal and vice versa, and water to the thirsty or fire to the cold. We have still, however, to show more fully how the inherent symbolism of instrumental performance is made public, adequate, permanent, and transmissible.

Before we come to that, however, it will be interesting to establish that our instrumental analysis of behavior corresponds closely to our concept of institution and its component parts. The above diagram contains as a definition of instrumental performance the items, objects, techniques, the coöperation and transmission, as well as situation. In concrete analysis this means that human beings achieve their ends by using artifacts within a definite environmental setting, by direct coöperation or else by the traditional coöperation which means re-enactment of established empirical processes; and obviously, in all this, they followed the learned traditional techniques of their culture. Comparing this with the previous diagram (page 125), we can see that material apparatus corresponds directly to environmental situation and objects used. Techniques and rules of coöperation would be placed under our heading of *norms*. The concept of coöperation obviously refers to personnel, and so does that of traditional learning, since this can only be obtained through the fact of organization. Where would we place our two concepts of Drive (1) and Drive (2)? It might be added here in parentheses that the splitting of the drive into two components is a necessary device of abstraction. It illustrates the fact that the drive is a necessary presupposition of the instrumental, as well as of any simple vital sequence. In reality, however, we have to remember always that the drive is integral and that it works right through the sequence, controlling all its phases and invariably leading to the final stage, that of satisfaction. Our device of splitting this concept, however, illustrates the fact that all the elements in the instrumental performance receive their value because the initial stages of the drive lead the conditioned organism to the instrumental outfit, endowing it, thus, with cultural value. Drive (2), based directly on organic impulse, and reinforced by satisfaction, supplies the reinforcement to all the instrumental elements by being inseparably linked up with Drive (1).

We have now seen that what we have defined as charter, that is, the traditionally established values, programs, and principles of organized behavior, correspond once more, fully and directly, to our concept of drive, insofar as this is culturally reinterpreted. This cultural reinterpretation, again, means that the drive operates in a two-fold manner, first by the establishment of the value of the apparatus, and of the instrumental quota in the performance, and then by reappearing as a culturally determined Drive (2), in leading to the culturally reinterpreted act of consummation. To the entry of activities there corresponds clearly the instrumental series as a whole, insofar as it is observed in actual execution and not analyzed into its constituent factors. The difference, to make it quite clear once more, is that we observe in field-work the constituent factors of the series in their ideal, traditionally defined form. In actual performance, we study them with all the inherent deviation, imperfections, and occasional failures. The concept of function, as it appears on our earlier diagram, obviously is the linkage between satisfaction and drive. More fully, since our institutional diagram refers not to a single performance, but to the sum total of instrumentalities connected with all drives of a certain type, function would mean here the range of instrumentalities assessed with reference to the complex drives and the manifold satisfactions of a need. To make our argument here clear, let us once more project the analysis onto a new diagram in terms of stimulus and response psychology and, more concretely, of our application thereof through the concept of instrumentally implemented vital sequences.

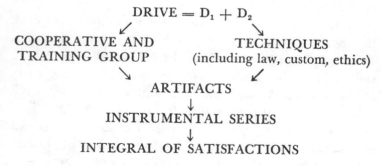

$$\text{DRIVE} = D_1 + D_2$$

COOPERATIVE AND TRAINING GROUP   TECHNIQUES (including law, custom, ethics)

ARTIFACTS

INSTRUMENTAL SERIES

INTEGRAL OF SATISFACTIONS

We can rapidly draw a few conclusions important in any cultural analysis. Our diagrammatically formulated theory of instrumental sequences shows that the concept of drive can never be eliminated from any cultural performance, simple or complex. The reason why an artifact, a habit, or an idea or belief becomes permanently incorporated into a culture, primitive or civilized, is because it enters an instrumental series at one stage or other, and because it remains as an integral part of an instrumental series. The animal psychologist teaches us one important fact: a habit which is not reinforced becomes unlearned, "extinguished." It disappears. We can apply this fully to culture. No crucial system of activities can persist without being connected, directly or indirectly, with human needs and their satisfaction. The understanding of any cultural element must imply, among other things, the statement of its relationship, instrumental or direct, to the satisfaction of essential needs, whether these be basic, that is biological, or derived, that is, cultural. When a habit ceases to be rewarded, reinforced, that is, vitally useful, it simply drops out. This is, in other words, our criticism of "survival," meaningless traits, irrelevant form, and similar concepts used as illegitimate devices of argument in the reconstructive work of certain evolutionary or diffusionist theories.

Another conclusion is that, once formally established, the instrumentally extended vital series become stringent. We find that the educational or biological approach to the study of the formation of personality, and the entry of the individual into various organized systems of activities, is an essential part of all cultural understanding. This analysis could be, again, extended so as to show that all incorporation of an individual organism into an instrumental series carries with it a legal element. The imperfection in technical performance, the disobedience of the rules of coöperation, and the mishandling of objects or people in short, provide ultimate punishment of the organism by the miscarriage of the instrumental sequence. The punishment received by the organism within an instrumental sequence from the material apparatus is probably the earliest and most effective disciplinary measure provided by all cultural activities for the regulation of man's behavior. Again, we see that the economic principle, in terms of value achieved through effort, as well as through the circumstance that the instrumental part of our series is the one which is most variable, that is, interchangeable, is once more put on the map of cultural analysis.

The complex, cumbersome, materially as well as socially founded apparatus constitutes the means through which and in which human beings satisfy the constant basic needs. This apparatus also allows them to develop new needs and, as we have seen from our concept of two-fold drive, it leads toward the creation of new drives and new desires. This apparatus has to be carried on as a whole for the benefit of that group which exercises it conjointly. It has to be continued with full efficiency, or else the group whose needs—and that refers even to the basic organic ones—could not be fulfilled by mere animal subsistence on the environment, would not survive.

It will be well to add one more generalization. In biological evolution the concept of the survival of the fittest and the struggle for existence still retains its fundamental importance, in spite of certain corrections which were inflicted upon it by Darwin's followers. Prince Peter Kropotkin was quite right in pointing out that mutual aid between individuals of a coöperative community is the dominant concept, while the struggle between the individuals for survival can not be applied to human societies as a whole. We could not intelligently and with any chance of documentary evidence apply the concept of struggle for existence to primitive communities, certainly not in the sense of assuming a perpetual state of warfare, of extermination of weaker groups and the expansion of stronger ones at the expense of those defeated or destroyed.

We can, however, apply the concept of survival value to cultures. This probably would not be coupled here with any concept of struggle, but rather with that of competition, within cultures and between cultures. We could affirm that the failure within any culture as regards instrumental efficiency, artifacts, coöperation, or symbolic accuracy, would inevitably lead to the gradual extinction of the whole cultural apparatus.

We might add that the concept of contact diffusion is very useful here. A decaying culture would mean reduction in numbers, an inability of adaptation, and a partial return from the cultural to the animal status. Since probably, however, culture was developed simultaneously among several groups, we could assume that a deficiency of one culture could be remedied either by the incorporation of the deficient group into the more efficient culture, or by the exchange or adoption, in short, the diffusion, of certain devices from the higher to the lower level of culture. However this may be—and here, as ever, we avoid any too concrete and specific reconstructive visions—the principle that certain organically determined efficiencies of the cultural apparatus can be posited as the determining factors of its stability, vitality, chances for organization, and development, must be assumed as the basis of the functional treatment of culture as the gradually developing system of adequate adaptations of the human organism, and of human groups to the satisfaction of basic needs and the gradual raising of the standard of living within a given environment.

THE FUNCTIONAL THEORY

I EMBRYOLOGY AND OBSTETRICS

FUNCTIONALISM AS A method is as old as the first stirrings of interest in alien, hence reputedly savage and barbarian, cultures, whether the interest might have come from a Greek historian like Herodotus, a French Encyclopaedist like Montesquieu, or a German Romanticist such as Herder. Any small contribution I may have made consists in writing out and pinning the label of functionalism on an existing body of doctrine, method, and interest; and in doing even that, I referred in my original article on the subject to no less than twenty-seven predecessors. Thus, perhaps, I have acted as accoucheur and godfather to the youngest baby in the anthropological litter of schools and I have continued to carry on the *maieutike techne* (obstetric art) in the training of younger students of the subject by the traditions of one great teacher, who liked to describe his art as that of a midwife. There was another great teacher who supplied the motto of functionalism, "by their fruits ye shall know them."

Functionalism, in so far as it has been present in every anthropological approach, is concerned with the clear understanding of the nature of cultural phenomena, before these are submitted to further speculative manipulations. What is the nature, the cultural reality of human marriage and the family, of a political system, an economic enterprise, or legal procedure? How can these facts be treated inductively so as to yield valid scientific generalizations? Is there any universal scheme applicable to all human cultures, that might be useful as a guide to fieldwork and as a system of coördinates in comparative study, whether historical, evolutionary, or merely aiming at the general laws of correspondence?

When E. B. Tylor inquired at the beginning of his great work on *Primitive Culture* into what religion was, in the widest sense of the term, or, in his own words, when he attempted a "minimum definition" of this subject, he was a genuine functionalist. So was Robertson Smith, when he recognized that the sociological dimension was indispensable for an understanding of primitive faith. Again, Sumner, in his attempts at an analysis and classification of early norms of behavior, represents an initial functional interest. Durkheim's discussion of the primitive type of division of social labor, and his analysis of religion and magic, are within the scope of the functional method. The famous memoir by which Tylor attempted to correlate various aspects of early kinship and economic life; K. Bücher's definition of primitive economics and of the relation between labor and rhythmic song; the work of Hutton Webster and H. Schurtz on age grades, sacred societies, and men's voluntary associations, and the relation of these groups to the political, religious, and economic structure of the community—one and all of these contributions are functional. I might add that the earliest types of effective field-work, such as the work of Charlevoix, Dobritzhofer, Sahagun or Dapper, were also functional in that they contained an appreciation not merely of isolated facts but of essential relations and bonds.

Some functional principles must be embodied in every theoretical treatment of cultural phenomena, as well as in every competent monograph on field-work. Else I be suspected, however, of indiscriminate benevolence culminating in a flabby eclecticism, I hasten to add that nonfunctional as well as anti-functional tendencies exist in anthropology. The field-worker with his eye exclusively on the exotic or picturesque is one example. The evolutionist, developing a theory of the origin of marriage and the family, but untroubled about any clear distinction between marriage, merely sexual conjugation, and a temporary liaison, is another case in point. The selection of such a phenomenon as the classificatory system of kinship terms and the handling of it as a survival, a record of what has been but is no more, shows how, by neglecting the functional analysis of vital linguistic phenomena, Morgan misdirected anthropological research for generations. Again, Graebner, rigging up a false or puerile analysis of culture in order to lay the foundation of what he regarded as a fool-proof world-wide diffusionism, has created an anti-functional approach of first-rate imbecility. He first of all assumes that it is possible to isolate single items from their cultural context. He defines, then, form as completely disconnected from function. Indeed, to him those qualities of form in an object alone matter, which are not connected with its uses and purpose. Hence to Graebner only those characteristics are methodologically relevant which can be shown to be culturally irrelevant.

Furthermore, he includes the concept of trait complex as an assortment of disconnected items. I submit that form is always determined by function, and that in so far as we can not establish such a determinism, elements of form can not be used in a scientific argument. I also submit that a concept of disconnected items, in a type of reality where we cannot introduce elements intrinsically related to each other, is useless.

II GENERAL AXIOMS OF FUNCTIONALISM

I WOULD SUGGEST that all experience in the field, as well as the scrutiny of the really important manifestations of organized human behavior, demonstrate the validity of the following axioms:

A. Culture is essentially an instrumental apparatus by which man is put in a position the better to cope with the concrete specific problems that face him in his environment in the course of the satisfaction of his needs.

B. It is a system of objects, activities, and attitudes in which every part exists as a means to an end.

C. It is an integral in which the various elements are interdependent.

D. Such activities, attitudes and objects are organized around important and vital tasks into institutions such as the family, the clan, the local community, the tribe, and the organized teams of economic coöperation, political, legal, and educational activity.

E. From the dynamic point of view, that is, as regards the type of activity, culture can be analyzed into a number of aspects such as education, social control, economics, systems of knowledge, belief and morality, and also modes of creative and artistic expression.

The cultural process, looked at in any of its concrete manifestations, always involves human beings who stand in definite relations to each other, that is, they are organized, and handle artifacts, and communicate with each other by speech or some other type of symbolism. Artifacts, organized groups, and symbolism are three dimensions of the cultural process that are closely related to each other. What is the type of this relationship?

Looking first at the material apparatus of culture, we can say that every artifact is either an implement or else an object of more direct use, that is, belonging to the class of consumers' goods. In either case, the circumstances as well as the form of the object are determined by its use. Function and form are related.

This relationship brings us at once to the human element, for the artifact has either to be eaten up, used up, or otherwise destroyed; or else it is produced in order to be manipulated as a tool. The social setting is always a man or a group handling their implements in a technical, economic pursuit; using a house conjointly, consuming the food which they have produced or gathered and prepared. In point of fact, no single item of material culture can be understood by reference to an individual alone; for wherever there is no coöperation, and such cases are hard to find, there is at least the one essential coöperation which consists in the continuity of tradition. The individual has to acquire his personal skill and the knowledge behind it from a member of the community already acquainted with skills, technique, and information; and he has also to receive or to inherit his material equipment.

What is the form and what is the function in sociological realities? Take a relation by blood, contiguity or contract: we have here two or more people who behave to each other in a standardized manner, and who do this invariably with reference to some part of the environment culturally defined, and with reference to some concerns in which items are exchanged, objects handled, and bodily movements coördinated. The form of sociological reality is not a figment or an abstraction. It is a concrete type of behavior characteristic of any social relationship.

In the same way in which the physicist or the chemist observes the movements of bodies, reactions of substances, or changes in the electromagnetic field, and registers the typical recurrent behavior of matter, force, and energy; so too the field-worker has to deal with recurrent situations and activities, and to register their canons or patterns. We could imagine a variety of cinematographic films of parental behavior showing the technology of nursing, fondling, and training, the ritual, as well as the everyday phases in which the sentiments between father, mother, and children are expressed and standardized. When we come to very rigidly defined behavior, such as in religious ceremonies, legal transactions, magical ritual, and a technological operation, a combined sound film would provide us with an objective definition of the form of sociological reality.

Here we can emphasize the first theoretical point, that in such an objective presentation of the sociological dimension, no line of demarcation can be drawn between form and function. The function of conjugal relations and of parenthood is obviously the culturally defined process of reproduction. The form in any specific culture is the manner in which it is done, and which differs in the technique of obstetrics, in the ritual of the couvade, and the mode of parent taboos and seclusions; of baptismal rites and of keeping the infant protected, sheltered, clad, clean, and nourished.

The second theoretical point is that it is impossible to isolate the material aspect of social behavior, or to develop a social analysis completely detached from symbolic aspects; and also that the three dimensions of cultural reality enter at every step of the process. A silent film would contain only part of the documentation, such as symbolism in ritual gesture, in sacramental implement, or in significant signs and conventional movements carried out by the participants. The most important aspect of symbolism, of course, is verbal, and here we know that a great deal of collateral comment, not necessarily contained in the performance itself, constitutes an indispensable additional documentation on the part of the field-worker.

What is the relation between form and function in symbolism? Were we to detach the mere phonetic reality of a word, or any other purely conventional characteristic of a material symbol of a gesture, it might appear that the link between form and function here is purely artificial; and since symbolism in its very essence is but the development of conventional acts for the coördination of concerted human behavior, the relation between form and function here is definitely artificial or conventional. The symbol is the conditioned stimulus, which is linked up with a response in behavior only by the process of conditioning. But in every piece of field-work this process ought to be an integral part of valid research. The context of the formative situation, on the other hand, always reveals the relation between the function of a symbolic act, verbal or manual, and certain physical processes linked up by biological causality.

The form in symbolism therefore, I submit, is not a word torn out of its context, a gesture photographed, or an implement put into a museum, but such an item studied dynamically reveals that it plays a part as a catalyzer of human activities, as a stimulus which releases responses in a chained reflex, in a type of emotion, or in a process of cerebration. In the form of a military command, "fire!" is the performance as a whole, more especially the behavior in *response* to the command, the social coördinate behavior as released by the conventional stimulus. Because the *dynamic* character of the stimulus lies in the response, the word "fire" written on a piece of paper and rediscovered in A.D. 3000 would mean nothing. That is not a cultural reality.

We have thus established that the totality of a cultural process involving the material substratum of culture, that is, artifacts; human social ties, that is, standardized modes of behavior; and symbolic acts, that is, the influences of one organism on another through conditioned stimulus reflexes; is a totality which we cannot cut up by isolating objects of material culture, pure sociology, or language as a self-contained system.

III FUNCTION DEFINED

THIS ANALYSIS will allow us to define the concept of function with greater precision. It is clear that we have to approach it through the concepts of use or utility and relationship.

In all activities we find that the use of an object as a part of technically, legally, or ritually determined behavior leads human beings to the satisfaction of some need. Fruits or roots are gathered, fish caught, animals hunted or trapped, cattle milked or slaughtered, so as to provide the raw materials of the human larder. These again are seasoned, prepared, and cooked so as to come on the table. All of this culminates in an individual or communal meal. The nutritive need controls an extreme multiplicity of processes. It is a commonplace to say that humanity advances on its belly, that you can keep the multitude satisfied by providing bread as well as circuses, and that the materialistic factor of satisfactory food supply is one of the determinants of human history and evolution. The functionalist only adds that the motives which control the parts of this process, and which become broken up into the passion for gardening and hunting, into the interest or greed for suitable exchange and marketing, into impulses of generosity and munificence, must all be analyzed with reference to the main drive, that of hunger. The integral function of all the processes which constitute the cultural commissariat of a community is the satisfaction of the primary biological need of nutrition.

If we turn to another activity, that of the production and maintenance of fire, we once more could refer it to its

primary uses in cooking and in keeping up the environmental temperature, as well as an implement in certain
technical processes. A variety of attitudes, religious and
secular, legal and technical, which center around fire, the
hearth, the sacred flame, can all be related to its main
biological functions.

Take the human dwelling. It is a physical object, a construction of logs or boughs, of animal skins, snow or stone.
Having form, however, the technology of its structure, as
well as its divisions, component parts, and furniture, are
related to domestic uses which are linked up to the organization of the household, the family group, its depend-
ents and servants. Here once more, the integral function
of the object must be kept in mind in studying the various
phases of its technological construction as well as the elements of its structure.

What is the function of kinship terms, primary and
derived, individual and collective, descriptive and classificatory? I maintain that in this case the study of the initial
situation of kinship, that is, of the small group surrounding the infant and including him as a sociological acquisi-
tion to the community, would reveal that the earliest
function of kinship terms is to provide the infant with a
sociological control of its environment through articulate
speech. This, incidentally, implies the assertion that the
context of the formative situation in these linguistic symbols, and in human language in general, is essentially
sociological and also individual. The non-individual or
classificatory meanings of kinship terms are acquired
through a series of consecutive extensions. The functional
approach to this phenomenon, therefore, implies that all
those contexts in which the symbolic aspect of kinship is
successively worked out, will be studied by drawing in
linguistics, social behavior, and material setting. When we

say social behavior we mean legal norms, economic services, and any ritual that accompanies the stages in the
development of an individual from infancy into membership in the widest kinship group, the clan, and the tribe.
It would be easy to show that various material objects usually labelled "money," "currency," or "symbolic wealth,"
would have to be studied also within the context of systems
of exchange, production, and consumption. And the same
refers to the study of a magical formula or gesture, which
once more must not be torn out of its context, but related
to its function.

THE ROUGH APPROACH TO
FUNCTIONALISM

THE PERSISTENT teaching of experience in field-work, as well as any piece of comparative theoretical investigation, does, and inevitably has, led the anthropologist into the realization that cultural phenomena are related. The ties between an object and the human beings who use it, between the technique, individual and social, and legal ownership, as well as the economics of production, the relation between the human dwelling and the members of the household who occupy it, are so obvious that they never have been completely overlooked nor yet clearly seen! For, proverbially, nothing is as difficult to see as the obvious. If functionalism were merely the tendency to regard "magic and economic attitudes as interlocking," to realize that they are a part of social structure and that we must always correlate further and further, it would indeed be that theoretical lapse into scientific totalitarianism of which it has been often accused. There is no doubt also that in science we must isolate as well as establish relations. Functionalism would lead us into the bog of relating and counter-relating objects if it could not point out some isolates or units which contain natural limits of coördination and correlation. I submit that such natural isolates do exist, and that they should be made the foundation of any sound culture analysis.

The functional isolate that I have labelled Institution differs from the culture complex or trait-complex, when defined as "composed of elements which stand in no necessary relation to each other," in that it does postulate such a necessary relationship. In fact, the functional isolate is concrete, that is, can be observed as a definite social grouping. It has a structure universally valid for all types of isolates; and it is a real isolate in so far as we can not only enumerate its abstract factors, but also concretely draw a line around it. Functionalism would have no true claim to deal with culture in its fundamental aspects, such as educational, legal, economic, or pertaining to knowledge, primitive or developed, and religion, unless it were able to analyze and thus define each, and relate them to the biological needs of the human organism.

Functionalism would not be so functional after all, unless it could define the concept of function not merely by such glib expressions as "the contribution which a partial activity makes to the total activity of which it is a part," but by a much more definite and concrete reference to what actually occurs and what can be observed. As we shall see, such a definition is provided by showing that human institutions, as well as partial activities within these, are related to primary, that is, biological, or derived, that is, cultural needs. Function means, therefore, always the satisfaction of a need, from the simplest act of eating to the sacramental performance in which the taking of the communion is related to a whole system of beliefs determined by a cultural necessity to be at one with the living God.

V THE LEGITIMATE ISOLATES
OF CULTURAL ANALYSIS

I MAINTAIN that if you were to take any trait of material culture, or select any custom, that is, standardized way of behavior, or any idea, it would be possible to place it within one or more organized systems of human activity. Thus, if you were to chance upon a group of natives making fire by friction, it could be either the kindling of a domestic fire for cooking or warmth; or just to establish the first kindling of the hearth. In either case, the fire thus kindled would be an integral part of the domestic institution; but it might also be a campfire, part of an organized hunting, fishing, or trade expedition. It might also be a children's game. As a mere technological process, fire-making has also its tradition of knowledge, skill, and in many cases organized coöperation. If we were to study it either as a manual performance, or in the process of traditional continuity of the performance, we would also have to refer it to an organized group of people connected with the transmission of this type of activity.

An implement again has a purpose, a technique, and it can always be referred to the organized group, the family, the clan, or the tribe, within which the technique is cultivated and embodied in a statement of technical rules. A word, or types of words, such as a kinship terminology, the sociological expressions for rank, authority, and legal procedure, have also obviously their matrix of organization, of material equipment, and of ultimate purpose, without which no group is organized. Were we to take any custom, that is, standardized form of behavior, it would be either a skill, a mode of physiological behavior in eating, sleeping, transport, or game; or else it might express directly or symbolically a sociological attitude. In every case this again belongs to an organized system of activities. I would challenge anyone to mention any object, activity, symbol, or type of organization, which could not be placed within one institution or other, although some objects belong to several institutions, playing specific parts in each.

VI THE STRUCTURE OF AN INSTITUTION

To be quite concrete, let me first suggest that it is possible to draw up a list of types; thus, for instance, the family, an extended kinship group, a clan, or a moiety, constitute one type. They are all connected with the chartered and legalized modes of human reproduction. The charter always corresponds to a desire, a set of motives, a common purpose. This is embodied in tradition or granted by traditional authority. In marriage, the charter, that is, the body of constitutional rules, consists in the law of marriage and descent, these two being intrinsically related. All the principles by which the legitimacy of off-spring is defined, the constitution of the family, that is, the direct reproductive group stating the specific norms of coöperation—all this constitutes the charter of the family. The charter varies from community to community, but it is a piece of knowledge which must be obtained in field-work and which defines the domestic institution in each culture. Independent of such a system of fundamental or constitutional rules, we still must know more fully the personnel, that is, the membership of the group, the seat of authority and the definition of functions within the household. The specific rules, technological and legal, economic and workaday, are other constituent factors to be studied by the field-worker.

The family life, however, centers around the domestic hearth; it is physically determined by the type of dwelling, the outfit of domestic implements, furniture, and also the sacred objects associated with any magical or religious cult carried out by the household as a group. We have here, therefore, such elements as charters, personnel, the norms of coöperation and conduct, and material setting. These data being assembled, we still have to obtain a full concrete description of life within the household, with its seasonal variation, its routine of day and night, and also with the full consideration of actual deviations from the norms.

In a community where, over and above the family in the narrower sense, there exists one or more types of extended kinship group, analysis in field and theory along the same lines would show that such a group has also its charter in the customary law of an extended household. It has its rules of give-and-take between the component members, it has a widened personnel, and the material substratum of a spacially contiguous compound, joint enclosure, common symbolic hearth, main as well as dependent dwellings, and also certain objects used in common, as against those pertaining to component families.

The charter of the clan is given in the mythology of a common ancestor, and in the unilateral emphasis on an extended kinship affiliation.

In all parts of the world we would find also municipal groupings. Whether we deal with a nomadic horde, or a local group of Australian aborigines, Andamanese, Californians or Fuegians, we find that people who live contiguously have exclusive claims to a definite portion of territory, and carry out conjointly a number of activities in which direct man-to-man coöperation is indispensable, and tends to become organized. However rudimentary such organization might be, it implies a statement of the group's claim to its lands. This very often is associated with mythological and religious, as well as the strictly legal, claims. Into the charter, therefore, enters the definition of individual rights to municipal citizenship, the claim of a group as a whole to its land and a whole set of historical, legendary, and mythological tradition that weld the group into a unit grown out of its soil. In a small farcical form, such a charter has been refabricated in the *Blut und Boden* doctrine of modern Naziism.

The local group has also its personnel, with a more-or-less developed central authority, with differentiations or partial claims of individual land tenure, and of divisions in communal function, that is, services rendered and privileges claimed. All the detailed rules of land tenure, the customary norms of communal enterprise, the definition of seasonal movements, especially as regards occasional gatherings of the municipality as a whole, constitute the rules which define the normative aspect of this institution. The territory, buildings, public utilities, such as paths, springs, waterways, constitute the material substratum of this group. The territorial principle may serve as a basis for even wider or provincial units, in which several municipalities are united. Here also, I would suggest the field-worker would have to investigate the existence of a traditional charter, that is, *raison d'être,* and historical antecedents of such a grouping. He would have to describe its personnel, the customary law governing the joint activities of such a provincial or regional group, and the way they control their territory and wealth and the implements of their coöperation, whether these be weapons, ceremonial objects, or symbols.

The tribe is, obviously, the unit at which we arrive in extending our territorial progress into ever-widening modes of organization and coöperative activities. Here, however, I would suggest that this concept has been used with an ambiguity and confusion of principle somewhat prejudicial to an ethnographic terminology. I submit that a distinction must be made between the tribe, in the cultural sense of the word, and the tribe as a politically organized unit. The tribe as the widest carrier of a unified culture consists of a group of people who have the same tradition, customary law, and techniques, and have throughout the same organization of smaller groups, such as the family, the municipality, the occupational guild or the economic team. The most characteristic index of tribal unity, I, personally, see in the community of language; for a common tradition of skills and knowledge, of customs and beliefs, can only be carried on conjointly by people who use the same tongue. Coöperative activities, in the full sense of the word, are again possible only between people who can communicate with each other by language.

A tribe-nation, as I propose to designate this institution, is not necessarily politically organized. Political organization implies always a central authority with the power to administer regarding its subjects, that is, to coördinate the activities of the component groups; and when we say power, we presuppose the use of force, spiritual and physical alike. I suggest that the tribe in the second sense of the word, the widest political grouping or the tribe-state, is not identical with the tribe-nation. I fully agree with the results of Professor Lowie's analysis, in his book on the origin of the state, that political groupings are absent among the most primitive cultures known to ethnographic observation. The cultural groupings, however, are there.

The charter of the tribe-nation can always be found in those traditions that deal with the origins of a given people, and that define their cultural achievements in terms of heroic ancestral performance. Historical legends, genealogical traditions, and historical explanations used to account for the differences between their own culture and that of neighbors, would enter into this, too. The charter of the tribe-state on the other hand, is that unwritten but never absent constitution of authority, power, rank and chieftainship. The personnel in a cultural group would deal with problems of stratification or its absence, of rank, of age-grades running through the culture, and obviously also of its regional subdivision. When the regional subdivision differs sensibly in culture and language, we might be faced by the dilemma as to whether we deal with several tribe-nations, or with a federation in the cultural sense of autonomous cultural subdivisions. There is no difficulty in seeing what the personnel of the tribe-state is. It obviously would involve the questions of a central authority, chieftainship, council of elders, as well as methods of policing and military force. Here also the question of tribal economics, taxation, treasury, and the financing of tribal enterprises would come in. As regards the material substratum, that of nationality can be defined only in terms of the differential character of this substratum, in so far as it separates one culture from all others. In the tribe-state the territory politically controlled, the weapons of defence and aggression, as well as the tribal wealth pooled and used in common for the political control, military and administrative, would enter the picture.

Following a line of inquiry divorced from the territorial principle, we could put on our list of institutions any organized and crystallized groupings by sex and age. Here, obviously, we would not include such institutions as the family, where the sexes complement each other and co-operate, but institutions such as the so-called totemic sex groupings, differential age-grades, and organized initiation camps for women and men, respectively. When we have an age-grade system referring only to the men of the community we can say that both sex and age enter as differential principles, and are one-sidedly institutionalized. I doubt whether anyone would find difficulty in defining the charter or norms and material apparatus entering here. Male associations, that is, secret societies, clubs, bachelors' houses, and such like, can be included in the concept of institutions without difficulty. Let me remind you that each such grouping has also its legal and mythological charter, and that this implies a definition of its personnel and its norms of behavior, and that each of them has a material embodiment, a place of reunion, some wealth, and some specific ritual and instrumental apparatus.

A large group of institutions can be included in a wide class, which we might label occupational or professional. The various aspects of culture, that is, the various types of activity such as education, economics, the administration of law, magical performance and religious worship, may or may not be embodied in specific institutions. Here the evolutionary principle cannot be dismissed from the functional theory. For there is no doubt that in the course of human development the needs for economic organization, for education, for magical or legal services, have been increasingly satisfied by specialized systems of activities. Each group of specialists becomes more and more closely organized into a profession. Nevertheless, the subject of discovering the earliest type of occupational groups is fascinating, not only for the student interested in wide schemes of evolution, but also for the field-worker and the comparative student. Few anthropologists would disagree that in magic and religion, or in certain technical skills and types of economic enterprise, we see organized groups at work, each with its traditional charter, that is, the definition of how and why they are qualified to cooperate; each with some form of technical or mystic leadership in division of functions; each with its norms of behavior and each, of course, handling the specific apparatus involved.

THE CONCEPT OF FUNCTION

I SUGGEST THAT THE concept can and must be fitted into our institutional analysis. The function of the family is the supply of citizens to a community. Through the contract of marriage the family produces legitimate offspring, that have to be nurtured, given the rudiments of education and later equipped with material goods, as well as with appropriate tribal status. The combination of morally approved cohabitation, not only in matters of sex but also for companionship and parenthood, with the law of descent, that is, the charter of the institution with its full social and cultural consequences, gives us here the integral definition of this institution.

The function of the extended family I would define in terms of a more effective exploitation of communal resources, of the strengthening of legal control within a narrow and well-disciplined unit of the community, and in many cases of an increased political influence, that is, greater safety and efficiency, of well-disciplined local units. The function of clanship I see in the establishment of an *additional network of relations* cutting across the neighborhood groupings and providing a new principle in legal protection, economic reciprocity, and the exercise of magical and religious activities. The clan system adds, in short, to the number of those personal bonds which reach across a whole tribe-nation, and allow for a much wider personal exchange of services, ideas, and goods, than would be possible in a culture organized merely on the basis of extended families and neighborhood groups. The function of the municipality I see in the organization of public

services and the conjoint exploitation of territorial resources, in so far as this has to be carried out by coöperation, but within the limit of day-by-day accessibility.

Organized sexual divisions within the tribe, as well as
age-grades, subserve the differential interests of human
groups, physically defined. If here we try to understand
primitive conditions by what is happening in our own
society we see that being a man or a woman, respectively,
entails certain natural advantages and also handicaps, and
that a community in which the sexes combine may be able
better to exploit the advantages and compensate the deficiencies between the two natural segments. The same
refers to age. Age-grades define the rôle, the potentialities,
and the type of services best rendered by each grade, and
apportion the reward in terms of status and power. There
is little to be said about the function of each professional
group. It is defined in terms of specific service and adequate reward. Here again the anthropologist who includes
contemporary savagery in his interest in primitive peoples
can see the same integral forces operating in the combination of people, who render the same services, share the
same interests and look after the customary reward,
whether in the conservative spirit of the primitive, or in
the competitive mood of our present day revolutionary
society.

This type of functional analysis is easily exposed to the
accusation of tautology and platitude, as well as to the
criticism that it implies a logical circle, for, obviously, if
we define function as the satisfaction of a need, it is easy
to suspect that the need to be satisfied has been introduced
in order to satisfy the need of satisfying a function. Thus,
for instance, clans are obviously an additional, one might
say, supererogatory type of internal differentiation. Can we
speak of a legitimate need for such differentiation, espe-

cially when the need is not ever present; for not all communities have clans, and yet they go on very well without them.

I would like first to say that here I am not too dogmatic myself. I would rather suggest that a concept of function in this sense, that is, as a contribution towards a more closely knit social texture, towards the wider and more penetrating distribution of services and goods, as well as of ideas and beliefs, might be useful as a reorientation of research along the lines of the vitality and cultural utility of certain social phenomena. I would also suggest that in cultural evolution we might introduce the concept of the struggle for maintenance, not of individual organisms nor yet of human groups, but rather of cultural forms. This also might be useful as a principle in assessing the chances of diffusion. Thus I suggest the concept of function with reference to certain wide, separate institutional groups, primarily as a heuristic device.

THE THEORY OF NEEDS

THE CONCEPT, HOWEVER, receives its strongest support from another type of consideration. If we can arrive at the assessment of what the various needs are; which of them are fundamental, and which are contingent; how they are related, and how the contingent cultural needs arise, we may reach a fuller and more precise definition of function, and show the real importance of this concept. Here I would like to suggest that we must take our stand on two axioms: first and foremost, that every culture must satisfy the biological system of needs, such as those dictated by metabolism, reproduction, the physiological conditions of temperature, protection from moisture, wind, and the direct impact of damaging forces of climate and weather, safety from dangerous animals or human beings, occasional relaxation, the exercise of the muscular and nervous system in movement, and the regulation of growth. The second axiom in the science of culture is that every cultural achievement that implies the use of artifacts and symbolism is an instrumental enhancement of human anatomy, and refers directly or indirectly to the satisfaction of a bodily need. If we were to start with an evolutionary consideration, we could show that as soon as the human anatomy is supplemented by a stick or a stone, a flame or a covering wrap, the use of such artifacts, tools, and commodities not only satisfies a bodily need, but also establishes derived needs. The animal organism which creates a change in temperature by the use of shelter, permanent or temporary, of fire, protective or warming, of clothing or blanketing, becomes dependent on those items of the environment, on their skillful production and use, and on the coöperation which may be necessary in the handling of the material.

A new type of need, closely linked to the biological one and dependent upon it, but obviously implying new types of determinism, arises with the beginning of any cultural activity. The animal, which passes from nourishment obtained directly from environmental contact to food collected, preserved, and prepared, will starve if at any stage the cultural processes break down. New needs of an economic character have to be registered side by side with the purely biological necessity of nutrition. As soon as the gratification of sex impulses becomes transformed into permanent cohabitation, and the rearing of infants leads to a permanent household, new conditions are imposed, each of them as necessary to the preservation of the group as is any phase of the purely biological process.

Were we to look at any community, more or less primitive, or even fully civilized, we would see that everywhere there exists a tribal commissariat determined primarily by the nutritive needs of human metabolism, but in itself establishing new needs, technological, economic, legal, and even magical, religious, or ethical. And again, since reproduction in the human species does not take place by simple mating, because it is linked up with the necessity for prolonged nurture, education, and the first molding into citizenship, it imposes a whole set of additional determinants, that is, needs, which are satisfied by a regulated courtship, by the taboos of incest and exogamy, by preferential marriage arrangements; and as regards parenthood and kinship, by the system of counting descent, with all which that implies in coöperative, legal, and ethical relations. The minimum conditions of bodily survival, as regards inclemencies of the weather, are again satisfied by dress and habitation. The need of safety leads to physical arrangements within the house, as well as within human settlements as a whole, and also to the organization of neighborhood groups.

If we were to enumerate briefly the derived imperatives imposed by the cultural satisfaction of biological needs, we would see that the constant renewal of apparatus is a necessity to which the economic system of a tribe is a response. Again, human coöperation implies norms of conduct sanctioned by authority, physical force, or social contract. Here we have the response of various systems of control, primitive or developed. The renewal of the human personnel in every component institution, and in the cultural group as a whole, implies not only reproduction, but also systems of education. The organization of force and compulsion in the support of authority and defence is functionally related to the political organization within each institution and also later on in specific groupings, which we have defined as political units, or the prototype of the political state.

Further on, I think that we will have to admit that from the beginning of culture its transmission by means of symbolically framed general principles was a necessity. Knowledge, partly embodied in manual skills, but also formulated and centered in certain principles and definitions referring to material technological processes, has, too, an early pragmatic or instrumental causality, a factor which could not be absent even in the earliest cultural manifestations. Magic and religion can be, in my opinion, functionally interpreted as the indispensable complements to pure rational and empirical systems of thought and tradition. The use of language with reflection on the past, which is characteristic of all systematic thinking, would have early drawn the attention of human beings to the uncertainty of their purely intellectual predictions. The bridging of gaps in human knowledge and the rounding off of the big lacunæ in the appreciation of destiny and fate led man to the assertion of supernatural forces. Survival after death is probably one of the earliest mystical hypotheses, related perhaps to some deep biological cravings of the organism, but certainly contributing to the stability of social groups and towards the sense that human endeavors are not as limited as purely rational experience shows. Ideas which, on the one hand, assert that man can control some elements of chance, and on the other hand, imply that in nature itself there is a benevolent or vindictive response to human activities, contain the germs of more highly developed concepts, such as Providence, a moral sense in creation, and the goal of human existence. The functional explanation of art, recreation, and public ceremonials might have to refer to directly physical reactions of the organism to rhythm, sound, color, line and form, and to their combinations. It would also relate, in the decorative arts, to manual skills and perfection in technology, and link them up with religious and magical mysticism.

IX CONCLUSIONS

IT WILL BE CLEAR to anyone that I regard this as a mere tentative sketch. We still need a fuller and more concrete answer to the question whether cultural phenomena can be studied in so far as they integrate into natural isolates of organized activities. I think that the concept of institution, with a definite outline of its structure, with a complete list of its main types, supplies the best answer to the question.

The theory of needs and their derivation gives us a more definitely functional analysis of the relation between biological, physiological and cultural determinism. I am not quite certain whether my brief indication of what the function of each type of institution is, will remain final. I feel more convinced that I have been able to link up functionally the various types of cultural response, such as economic, legal, educational, scientific, magical and religious, to the system of needs—biological, derived, and integrative.

The functional theory, as here presented, claims to be the prerequisite for field-work and for the comparative analysis of phenomena in various cultures. It is capable of yielding a concrete analysis of culture into institutions and their aspects. If you imagine a field-worker supplied with such guiding charts, you will see that they might be helpful to him in isolating, as well as relating, the phenomena observed. It is meant primarily to equip the field-worker with a clear perspective and full instructions regarding what to observe and how to record.

Functionalism, I would like to state emphatically, is

neither hostile to the study of distribution, nor to the reconstruction of the past in terms of evolution, history or diffusion. It only insists that unless we define cultural phenomena in function as well as in form, we may be led into such fantastic evolutionary schemes as those of Morgan, Bachofen or Engels, or to piecemeal treatments of isolated items, such as those of Frazer, Briffault and even Westermarck. Again, if the student of distributions maps out fictitious and unreal similarities, his labors will be wasted. Thus functionalism definitely insists that as a preliminary analysis of culture it has its fundamental validity, and that it supplies the anthropologist with the only valid criteria of cultural identification.

SIR JAMES GEORGE FRAZER:
A BIOGRAPHICAL APPRECIATION

SIR JAMES GEORGE FRAZER:
A BIOGRAPHICAL APPRECIATION

INTRODUCTION

THE DEATH OF James George Frazer, on May 7, 1941, symbolizes the end of an epoch. Frazer was the last survivor of British classical anthropology. He represented better than any of our contemporaries that trend in humanism which sought inspiration from the comparative study of man for the understanding of the Greek, Latin, and Oriental cultures of antiquity. His name will perhaps be the last on the list of great humanists and classical scholars. Anatole France compared him with Montesquieu —a comparison not out of proportion, though perhaps out of focus. In the same, somewhat oblique, sense we might compare him to Jonathan Swift or to Francis Bacon, or even to Sir Thomas More. He certainly was in direct line of succession to such men as Tylor and Lord Avebury, Herder and Lessing, Winckelmann and Renan.

Frazer grew up, developed, and worked in an epoch in which scholarship was still possible in the sense of a leisurely pursuit of non-utilitarian learning and letters. His knowledge was vast and catholic. He could discuss physics with Lord Kelvin, Clerk Maxwell and J. J. Thompson; he knew a great deal of biology and other branches of natural science; he wrote essays and poetry in the manner of Addison and Lamb. He read his Homer in Greek, his Ovid and Virgil in Latin, and his Bible in Aramaic. His earlier life he spent at Trinity College, Cambridge, which he loved and where he flourished. The College was still the stronghold of scholarship to a Fellow, even as his home is a castle to the Englishman. The First World War, during which Frazer was expanding his *Golden Bough* into the final twelve-volume edition, dealt a mortal blow to scholarship, humanism, and *belles lettres*. The Second World War, which Frazer was not to survive, bids fair to eliminate the scholar as well as the gentleman from our civilization.

I THE PARADOX OF FRAZER'S
PERSONALITY AND WORK

As a man Frazer was not easy to understand; in some ways disappointing, full of contradictions and paradoxical turns of personality. In spite of his wide outlook and interests, he could be narrow and bigoted in theoretical views and general prejudices. Always ready to revise his opinions if these were contradicted by factual evidence, he could never brook personal contradiction or even engage in an argument. Passionately devoted to all that was strange, unusual and exotic in humanity, he was easily put out in meeting a stranger, and had great difficulty in adjusting to unusual personal contacts. Essentially humble, modest, and self-effacing, he achieved the highest formal honors and distinctions available to a man in his position.

His mundane glory was largely due to the activities of Lady Frazer, who took upon herself the management of his worldly career. Personally, Frazer despised and detested the limelight and glare of public acclamation, which he endured somewhat grudgingly but with resignation. Lady Frazer's word was the last one. Those of us who came to know the capable, energetic, though somewhat redoubtable life companion of Frazer became as devoted to her as to him. Orders, titles, and honorary degrees apart, she also coöperated with him, had his books translated, and managed for him his extensive correspondence and his relations with other scholars. With all this Lady Frazer was unquestionably a puzzling element to most of Frazer's friends as well as in his position in the academic world.

I knew Frazer for the last thirty-one years of his life. I was able to follow many of his personal relations with fellow anthropologists. I tried to understand his method of approaching problems, of dealing with evidence, and of developing his thoughts and theories. I know that through his personal contacts as well as his work he inspired many, perhaps most of modern thinkers and writers in anthropology, social science, and humanism. Yet he had always great difficulty in coming to grips with a problem in personal conversation. The great humanist was seldom able to adapt to human intercourse, in the ordinary give and take of a true teacher. It was always necessary to wait for the inspired moments in his conversation when he could improvise beautiful passages of prose, even as those we find in his written works. His genuine interest in every new fact discovered in field-work, and his ability to stimulate the field-worker by correspondence, is well known. The letters which I received from Frazer during my sojourns in New Guinea and Melanesia helped me more by suggestion, query and comment than any other influence.

He was a poor public speaker and an indifferent lecturer. He had a pronounced stage fright and preferred to read his lectures rather than deliver them *extempore*. In his literary work he formed clear-cut opinions and developed strong prejudices. He rejected, for instance, psychoanalysis and all that it meant. He could never be persuaded to read anything by Freud or his school, in spite of the fact that Freud's anthropological contributions are based on Frazer. Although he was an admirer and follower of Robertson Smith, he never came fully to appreciate the French sociological school of Durkheim, who developed Robertson Smith's social approach to religion.

Frazer completely avoided controversy and public discussion. Andrew Lang's typically buccaneering review of *The Golden Bough*—in which Frazer's theories were ridiculed as the "vegetable" or "Covent Garden" school of anthropology—so deeply upset and irritated Frazer that, as he told me, he had to interrupt his work on the subject for several months. After that experience Frazer never read adverse criticisms or reviews of his books.

Thus Frazer was not an instructor in a narrow sense of the word; he was not able dialectically to develop clear arguments and to defend them in controversy. Few of his purely theoretical contributions can be accepted as they stand. Yet, Frazer was and is one of the world's greatest teachers and masters.

Ethnographic field-work for the last half century or so has been under the spell of Frazer's suggestions. The work of Fison and Howitt, as well as of Spencer and Gillen in Australia; the famous Cambridge Expedition to Torres Straits led by A. C. Haddon in collaboration with W. H. R. Rivers, C. G. Seligman, and C. S. Myers; the African work of Junod, Roscoe, Smith and Dale, Torday, and Rattray—to mention only a few outstanding names— were carried on under the spiritual guidance of Frazer.

We have already mentioned Sigmund Freud, who, turning to anthropological evidence, took it from Frazer. The first and lasting contributions of the French School under the leadership of the dominant and domineering figure of Durkheim, and carried on by Hubert and Mauss, Lévy-Bruhl, Bouglé, and Van Gennep, are unthinkable without the inspiration and achievements of Frazer. In Germany, Wundt, Thurnwald, K. T. Preuss and many others have built on Frazer's foundations. In England writers like Westermarck and Crawley, Gilbert Murray and Jane Harrison, Sidney Hartland and Andrew Lang, take their cues and orientations from Frazer—whether they agree or disagree with him. The brilliant and stimulating figure of R. R. Marett of Oxford is the projection of Frazer's theories on a subtler, more analytic, but less original and comprehensive plane. Recently E. O. James still continues Frazer's tradition in his excellent contributions towards our understanding of present-day problems through anthropological analysis.

Frazer has influenced men like Anatole France, Bergson, Arnold Toynbee and O. Spengler. Frazer, more than any other writer, has made ethnographic evidence available as well as inspiring to a host of pioneer thinkers in history and psychology, in philosophy and ethics. This can be seen when the subjects with which anthropology has affected or inspired other studies are listed: taboo and totemism, magic and exogamy, forms of primitive religion and the development of political institutions. All these subjects have been first handled or most adequately treated by Frazer.

Thus in his personality, in his teaching, and in his literary achievement there is a touch of the paradoxical in the great Scottish scholar and his work. His enormous creative influence surprises sometimes even his devoted admirer when confronted by one of the naïve theoretical arguments from *The Golden Bough* or some other of his volumes. His inability to convince seems to contradict his power to convert and to inspire.

The explanation, as I see it, of Frazer's paradox lies in the specific combination of the qualities and defects of his mind. He is not a dialectician, not even perhaps an analytic thinker. He is, on the other hand, endowed with two great qualities: the artist's power to create a visionary world of his own; and the true scientist's intuitive discrimination between what is relevant and what adventitious, what fundamental and what secondary.

Out of his first virtue came his charm of style; his ability to reshape dull strings of ethnographic evidence into a dramatic narrative; his power to create visions of distant lands and of exotic cultures—which those of us who went there after reading Frazer are able best to appreciate.

Out of his scientific quality came his empirical sense. This led him—very often after he had formulated an insipid theory—to scour ethnographic literature and to extract from it evidence which often completely annihilates his own assumptions, but gives us the facts and the truths of magic or religion, of kinship or totemism in the real perspective within their relevant context, alive and palpitating with human desires, beliefs, and interests. Hence Frazer's uncanny gift of transforming crude, cumulative erudition into that wonderfully constructed architecture of evidence, where many of the theories, later put into words by others, are embodied. The long litanies of ethnographic data bore us to extinction in most writings of the classical evolutionary and comparative school. Transfigured by Frazer, they make *The Golden Bough* alive and vivid, *Totemism and Exogamy* interesting and instructive, and *Folk-lore in the Old Testament* an anthropological saga.

Frazer as a visionary lived in a very real and, to him, objective world. He molded his theories in the plastic material of evidence collected throughout the world and refashioned by him, so that without any exaggeration his facts demonstrate his true, albeit intuitive views. This explains why Frazer was always interested in field-work and seldom, if ever, in theories. He loved additions to his live world: the drama of human existence. He disliked any surgery done upon this world by theoretical criticism. Andrew Lang's satire was to Frazer not a personal insult, but a sacrilegious attack on Virbius, Osiris, and Baldur the Beautiful. Westermarck's theory of incest Frazer branded somewhat rudely as "bastard imitation of science."

It irritated him, not because he, Frazer, was contradicted, but because his beloved savages, as he knew them, would have found such a tame conception of incest essentially dull and unreasonable. Frazer, somewhat prudish in his reaction to psychoanalysis, insisted that his primitives must be both promiscuous and incestuous. With an almost maternal attitude of concern, he delighted in their pranks and pleasures, while regretting their naughtiness.

There was never anything small, mean, invidious, or personal in Frazer's reactions to criticism, in his own onslaughts or dislikes. I have never known anyone so genuinely modest, so humble in his love of evidence, and completely indifferent to praise or blame. Of all his qualities, it is perhaps this genuine devotion to the subject matter of his scientific and artistic interests, his complete disregard of any personal advancement, which made him one of the greatest artists in the plastic molding of theory in the live medium of primitive human existence.

II FRAZER'S POSITION
IN THE DEVELOPMENT OF
ETHNOLOGICAL THEORY

FRAZER IS THE REPRESENTATIVE of an epoch in anthropology which ends with his death. In all his directly theoretical contributions he is an evolutionist, interested in the "primitive," whether this refers to mankind at large, or to specific beliefs, customs and practices of contemporary "savages." He works by the comparative method, collecting and examining evidence from all parts of the world, at all levels of development, and in all cultures. The comparative method combined with the evolutionary approach implies certain general assumptions. Men are substantially similar. They develop gradually from a primitive level and pass through various stages of evolution. The common measure in their actions and their thoughts can be discovered by induction based on a vast survey of collated data. In this the concept of survival is essential to the evolutionist. It serves as the key for the understanding of continuity within transformation, and as a link between the various stages. What was a strong and flourishing belief at one level, becomes a superstition in the next higher one. Forms of marriage and kinship may become ossified into terminologies and survive as a linguistic usage, long after the practices of group marriage or promiscuity have ceased. As we move down the various levels of development we find the most primitive stage accessible, that is, the "origins" of human institutions, customs and ideas.

Frazer never developed any full theoretical statement of evolutionary principles. We cannot find in his work any precise definition of such concepts as "origins," "stage," "survival," nor yet any scheme which would allow us to assess how he imagined that evolution proceeded, or what were the driving forces of "progress." That he worked with all these concepts and constantly utilized the evolutionary as well as the comparative scheme of explanation, is obvious to the reader who has perused even a few pages in any of his works.

Frazer was essentially addicted to psychological interpretations of human belief and practice. His theory of magic, as the result of association of ideas; his three consecutive hypotheses about the origins of totemism in terms of belief in "external soul," "magical inducement of fertility," and in "animal incarnation," are essentially conceived in terms of individual psychology. Those who know his treatment of taboo, of the various aspects of totemism, of the development of magic, religion and science, will realize that, throughout, Frazer in his explicit theories is little aware of the problems of social psychology. He is, as already mentioned, fundamentally hostile to psychoanalysis, while behaviorism never enters his universe of discourse.

Although he was under the influence of Robertson Smith, the first modern anthropologist to establish the sociological point of view in the treatment of religion, Frazer never fully faced the sociological implications in any of his theoretical arguments. This is seen in his acceptance of Morgan's theory about primitive promiscuity and the development of marriage. Frazer never became aware of the social factor in folklore and mythology. To him magic and religion are still fundamentally "philosophies of life and destiny," as these might have occurred in the mind of a primitive, a savage, a barbarian, or an ancient Greek or Roman. He hardly follows in any of his theoretical comments Robertson Smith's principle that religion is a belief carried out by an organized group of people, and that it cannot be understood unless we treat a dogmatic system as a part of organized worship and of collective tradition.

Frazer is still inclined to relate taboo to "the ambition and avarice of chiefs and priests," who would use "animistic beliefs to buttress their power and accumulate their wealth." The fact that taboo is but a small part of primitive law or custom, and that this in turn cannot be explained either as "superstition" or "political and religious trickery" is never clearly explained in any of Frazer's arguments. The treatment of economics, art, and primitive epistemology in the fourth volume of *Totemism and Exogamy* is open to similar criticism.

An entirely different Frazer comes into action as soon as his thin introductory comments are over. He appears then as the cicerone guiding our steps on the deserts of Australia, among the tropical jungles of the Amazon or the Orinoco, on the steppes of Asia, or the highlands of Africa. His actual treatment of facts is supremely contextual; the various aspects of human culture and human concerns become interrelated; the occasional comments and the collateral evidence is illuminated with real insight into human motives. It would not be difficult to show that Frazer often comes near to developing a psychoanalytic insight into the unconscious and subconscious motives of human behavior. The proof of it can be seen in the ease with which Frazer's evidence has been used by Freud, Rank, and Róheim. In his ability to interpret motive and idea through deed and performance, in his conviction that acts can be trusted while words may be discredited, Frazer is essentially a behaviorist in the socio-

logical sense of the word. He certainly has the behavioristic tendency in documenting all psychological interpretations by forms of behavior.

Frazer's tendency to see anthropological facts as an integral part of human life in general, within the context
of the whole culture and even against the background of
landscape and natural environment, appears already, with
beauty and clarity alike, in his commentary to the translation of *Pausanias's Description of Greece* (1898). It
comes to full fruition in *The Golden Bough,* where the
somewhat unsatisfactory treatment of magic is followed
by a series of pictures, in which we see the magician as
chief and priestly king, the magician in his rôle of guard-
ian of the soil, war-lord and engineer of human and natural fertility.

Read one volume after another in the long series, and
you will find an encyclopædia of facts bearing upon the
problems of primitive relation to nature, early political
organization, taboo and other legal rules. Frazer's passion
to explore not only the main road, but also the byways
and perspectives opened at every step, implies and pro-
claims fuller and sounder theoretical interpretations than
those given explicitly by the author. His discussion of the
influence of sex upon vegetation contains a number of
ideas which later on were formulated by psychoanalysis,
but for which the facts were collected by Frazer with un-
erring intuition. The prohibitions and rules of conduct
which he lists as "taboos" contain a large material for the
study of primitive jurisprudence. Here again, following
Frazer, we perceive the principle that primitive law refers to acts, interests, and claims which on the one hand
refer to vital human concerns, food, sex, social position
and wealth, and which, on the other hand, necessitate restrictions and delimitations since they refer to a subject

matter in which man is tempted to transgress his customary rules.

The volumes concerned with agricultural ritual, the gods and goddesses of fertility, and the magical and religious interpretation of the yearly cycle, contain once more a live theory embodied in the presentation of facts. Frazer's insight in linking up ritual with the practical activities of food production tells us in so many words that religious and magical belief has always functioned as a principle of order, of integration, and of organization at primitive and at higher levels of human development. We see here magic not as a futile misconception, but rather as the crystallized optimism of hope carrying man along on his pursuits by the conviction that the desired end will be realized. We see also that sociologically the rôle of the early leader, the chief and the king, is not merely defined by his ability to exploit the commoner's superstition. Primitive leadership is seen to be the embodiment of man's conviction that the individual who is expert in the practical management of affairs can also manipulate the supernatural elements of chance and destiny. It is the pragmatic and intrinsic value of magic and religion which makes for their vitality and endurance.

Frazer's artistry, as well as his scientific sense in achieving a real synthesis from scattered and unrelated ethnographic evidence, appears at its best in his descriptive volumes on *Totemism and Exogamy*. Frazer describes totemic belief and ritual within the context of the social and political organization of each tribe. We find an outline of economics and social organization, of legal concepts and general beliefs, at times of military activities and ceremonial life. All this is prefaced, as a rule and wherever possible, by a picture of the landscape and an account of the environmental setting in which the natives live, and

from which they draw their livelihood. In many ways
Frazer's *Totemism and Exogamy* is about the best introductory reading for the young student of anthropology,
because it gives an easier, more attractive, and better integrated picture of a whole series of tribal cultures than any
book I know. Only recently has it been paralleled by G. P.
Murdock's *Our Primitive Contemporaries,* which comes
near in the quality of style and presentation to Frazer's
standard, and is more comprehensive as well as more precise as regards information.

The three volumes on *Folk-lore in the Old Testament*
and the later works of Frazer on immortality, *The Worship of Nature,* and *The Fear of the Dead,* are perhaps less
well contextualized than the descriptive chapters of *Totemism and Exogamy.* Yet even there Frazer's artistry and
his love of the integral and the comprehensive make the
works as instructive as they are pleasant to read.

Among the works of Sir James Frazer, the slender volume entitled *Psyche's Task* and republished later as *The
Devil's Advocate,* deserves special consideration. In one
way it is perhaps Frazer's most ambitious and most original contribution to the theory of human evolution. The
fundamental idea hinges on the relation between magical
and religious beliefs and some fundamental institutions
of mankind. Taking government, private property, marriage, and respect for human life, one after the other,
Frazer shows how far early "superstition" has contributed
towards their establishment and development. He deals
with moral concepts rather than with scientific ideas. The
distinctions between *good* and *bad,* between *superstition*
and *rational knowledge,* occur in most arguments. We are
even told "that these institutions have sometimes been
built on rotten foundations."

Yet even here Frazer's common sense leads him to a

caveat—and a contradiction. ".... There is a strong presumption that they (the institutions discussed) rest mainly on something much more solid than superstition. No institution founded wholly on superstition, that is, on falsehood, can be permanent. If it does not answer some real human need, if its foundations are not laid broad and deep in the nature of things, it must perish, and the sooner the better." The contradiction is clear. We are told in one place that these institutions sometimes rest on rotten foundations; and then, again, that their foundations have to be found somewhere broad and deep in the nature of things. The solution is indicated by Frazer himself. Such institutions as marriage, or law, or property, or government do "answer real human needs." Had Frazer inquired more fully into the nature of those needs, he might have, first and foremost, given us a correct theory of the real "origins" of human institutions and of such aspects of human culture as law, government, economics, and social organization. He would have discovered that forms of human organization which have endured from the very beginnings till our times, such as the family, kinship, the local group or municipality, and the state, correspond to definite needs of organized human life. He could then show, and show convincingly and adequately, why certain forms of magic and religion have contributed towards the permanence and the development of certain aspects of concerted human activities and of human groupings.

As it is, every one of the four chapters of *Psyche's Task*, suggestive and stimulating as it is, ends on a question-mark. After discussing the contributions of magic to government, we are told "that many peoples have regarded their rulers, whether chiefs or kings, with superstitious awe as beings of a higher order and endowed with mightier powers than common folk." Here Frazer's own evidence shows, as we have indicated, that authority, as the backbone of order and regulation, is indispensable in household, municipality, and tribe. The superstitious awe and respect given by the primitives to their chiefs is the by-product of the conviction that the leader leads in virtue of his power, his expert knowledge, and his *mana* or sanctity.

In discussing private property, we once more are told that superstitious fear operates "as a powerful motive to deter men from stealing." Yet stealing presupposes the existence of private property. Private property again, as the legally defined, exclusive right to use and to consume tools and goods respectively, is essential, and without such a principle there would occur a chronic chaos and dis-organization even in the simplest activities of primitive man. Once established, private property is protected by belief and magic, as well as by secular sanctions.

Marriage and the family correspond in their origins to the cultural need of transforming physiological reproduction into an organized, legally established form of coöp-erative life. This is the origin of marriage. The regulation of "sexual immorality whether in the form of adultery, fornication, or incest" is then carried on by various de-vices, magical belief being one of them. In this chapter Frazer is involved in a complex web of contradictions. As a follower of Morgan, McLennan and Bachofen, he as-sumes the existence of primitive promiscuity. He does not show us how marriage develops out of this original state. Yet obviously, and this we assume, the existence of mar-riage and the family form the beginnings of human cul-ture—an assumption now universally accepted by modern anthropology—and we cannot even inquire into the sanc-tions of early sexual morals. For under conditions of promiscuity or group marriage such morals would not exist.

Again, in the treatment of criminal law, Frazer tries to show that "the fear of ghosts, especially the ghosts of the murdered" has played an important part. Here again the modern anthropologist would insist that early criminal law was an indispensable prerequisite of the survival of primitive groups. The fear of ghosts of the murdered was the result of the sense of sin associated with murder. As such it probably fitted into the picture, but the real problem to an evolutionist is to discover how criminal law came into being. Then, and then only, can we understand all the beliefs which center around the transgression, and place them in their proper perspective.

With all this, the very problem posed by Frazer in this volume, the relation between belief and the organization of human institutions, is one of those which play a great rôle in modern anthropology.

CRITICAL ANALYSIS OF
SOME SPECIAL THEORIES

FRAZER'S BEST KNOWN contribution is his theory of magic in its relation to religion and science. Magic to Frazer is due to an essential conception of primitive man. It is the application, or rather misapplication, of the principles of association of ideas, and their transposition into a theory of natural processes. The two principles of magic are that like produces like, and that things which have been once in contact with each other continue to act on each other at a distance. Frazer designates these two principles as the laws of primitive magical outlook. "Though these laws are certainly not formulated in so many words, nor even conceived in the abstract by the savage, they are neverthe-less implicitly believed by him to regulate the course of nature quite independently of human will." The savage also applies these laws of nature after having discovered them and thus believes that he is able "to manipulate at pleasure certain natural forces."

In the light of our modern anthropological knowledge, this theory of magic, which also is a theory of the primitive outlook on the world, is untenable. We know now that primitive humanity was aware of the scientific laws of natural process. The most remarkable fact about this, however, is that Frazer, once more contradicting himself, formulates at the end of *The Golden Bough* the sound principle: ".... If under science we may include those simple truths, drawn from observation of nature, of which men in all ages have possessed a store," then it must have existed from the beginnings of time.

The contradiction is real because the whole introductory part to *The Golden Bough* is based on the essentially magical character of primitive outlook and primitive behavior. Yet throughout the presentation of facts, Frazer confirms not his untenable theory of magic as a misapplied principle of association, nor yet his evolutionary theory of three stages, but the sound and correct view that science, magic, and religion have always controlled different phases of human behavior. Frazer's own evidence demonstrates that they are co-existent and that they differ in substance, form, and function. The real problem is to define what they accomplish for man and wherein lie their psychological, social, and pragmatic foundations. Dip anywhere into *The Golden Bough* and follow the food-producing pursuits of primitives or peasants, whether hunting, fishing or agriculture, and you will find that they behave rationally on the basis of their scientific knowledge. Study the organization of Australians, Indians, or Polynesians, and you will see that their customs and principles of kinship and chieftainship are effective, that is, rational. You will find magic and religion occurring only with reference to such events as rain and sunshine, the hunters' luck, and the fishermen's chance, or else in touching the vital issues of human life where man can pray and propitiate his gods, but do very little by his knowledge and effort.

We could take Frazer's own evidence and the main outlines of principle contained in it, and we could formulate a theory of knowledge, magic, and religion fundamentally in accordance with Frazer's intuitive handling of his material, rather than with his explicitly stated views.

We would conclude with Frazer that man at all stages and in all climes is in possession of knowledge, empirically founded and logically handled. Even the simplest techniques of primitive man, his production of fire, implements and dwellings, imply the knowledge of material and the procedure of shaping and using it. They are fundamentally rational, since they are adequate. The primitive Australian knows his environment, the habits of the animals which he hunts, and the plants which he collects, since without such knowledge he would starve to death. In food collecting, hunting, fishing, and the production of weapons and utensils he is guided by his knowledge, which makes him coördinate rationally the concerted efforts of the team. Knowledge, indeed scientific knowledge, is always man's primary guide in his relation with the environment. It is his steady standby in all vital concerns. Without knowledge and without strict adherence to knowledge, no culture could survive. This is, then, the backbone of culture from the beginning onwards. Socially, expert knowledge and the mastery of technique are also at the basis of leadership and prominence. The man who knows how to organize a party and direct it in hunting, travelling, the shifting of the camp, and the distant trading expedition, is the natural leader. Thus as we know already, the problem of earliest government cannot be solved merely by reference to magic, religion, or any other "superstition." It has to take into account man's knowledge, man's pragmatic interests and the organization of these into collective performance.

Magic, as the belief that by spell and rite results can be obtained, enters as a complementary factor. It always appears in those phases of human action where knowledge fails man. Primitive man cannot manipulate the weather. Experience teaches him that rain and sunshine, wind, heat and cold, cannot be produced by his own hands, however much he might think about or observe such phenomena. He therefore deals with them magically.

Primitive man has but the most elementary knowledge

of conditions of human health and illness. Emotionally and pragmatically he strongly resents the occurrence of disease. A mystical theory that the malice of other men can produce illness is strongly suggested by man's psychology and by his social relations. In many ways the explanations given by the theory of witchcraft and sorcery are serviceable, in that they translate the inexorable decrees of destiny into manipulations of human malice. The sick man, primitive or civilized, wants to feel that something can be done. He craves for miracles, and the conviction that what has been produced by a malicious sorcerer can be counteracted by a more powerful and friendly witch-doctor, may even assist the organism to resist illness through the belief that something effective is being done.

Magic, including sorcery, has thus its practical as well as social characteristics, which allow us to explain its persistence. Psychologically, magic in all its forms implies the optimistic attitude that through rite and spell something is being achieved in taming chance and restoring luck. The form of rite and spell closely corresponds to this positive, pragmatic function. It is always the enactment of the desired end in word and act. We can here reformulate Frazer's theory: it is not the association of ideas, that like produces like or that contact persists, but the affirmation and enactment of desired ends and results, which form the psychological basis of magic. Socially, magic as the spiritual counterpart of leadership helps to integrate the acting group through discipline and the introduction of order. In agriculture the magician becomes the leader, not so much because of the superstitious reverence which he inspires, but because he gives the workers the guarantee that if they obey his taboos and his injunctions, his magic will add a quota of supernatural benefits to the practical results of their efforts. The magic of war again, inspiring the fighters with belief in victory, makes their courage more effective and allows leadership to be followed with fuller enthusiasm.

The distinction between religion and magic is perhaps not so much founded, as Frazer would like us to assume, in an essentially different attitude of man towards the entire universe. To Frazer magic is the direct coercion of natural forces by man; religion is the propitiation of divinities by the believer. The difference between the two, however, is to be found first in the subject matter: religion refers to the fundamental issues of human existence, while magic always turns round specific, concrete, and detailed problems. Religion is concerned with death and immortality, with the worship of natural forces in an integral general manner, with the tuning up of man to the rulings of Providence. Providence may appear at a primitive level as the system of totemic species, that is, the animals, plants and natural forces that affect man's existence most profoundly. Or else Providence may be enshrined in the pantheon of nature gods and goddesses. Or again it may be apprehended as a creative principle, the primitive All-Father or the High God of monotheistic religions.*

In its dogmatic structure, religion always presents itself as a system of belief defining the place of man in the universe, the provenience of man, and his goal. Pragmatically, religion is necessary to the average individual to overcome the shattering disruptive anticipation of death, of disaster, and of destiny. It solves these problems through the belief in immortality or in a peaceful dissolution of man in the universe or his reunion with divinity. Socially, since religion is always the core of civilization and the main-

* The text from this point to the end of the book did not have the benefit of final revision by Professor Malinowski. [Ed.]

spring of moral values, it becomes closely associated with every form of organization at lower and at higher levels. Within the family we find beliefs related to ancestor worship. The clan with its worship of totemic forebears, animal or human, functions as a religious congregation. We find local cults of villages, cities, and municipalities. Religion often becomes also the center of political states and empires.

Thus science, magic and religion are differentiated by subject matter, by the type of mental processes, by social organization, and by their pragmatic function. Each has its own clearly distinct form. Science is embodied in technology, based on observation and contained in theoretical precepts and later on, systems of knowledge. Magic appears as a combination of ritual, act, and spoken spell. It is revealed to man not through observation and experience, but in mythologically founded miracles. Religion takes the form of public or private ceremonial, prayer, sacrifice and sacrament.

In all this we find that evolution, as a metamorphosis of one type of belief or activity into an entirely different one, is not acceptable. We have to assume here, as in many other evolutionary problems, the existence of all the fundamental principles of human thought, belief, custom, and organization from the very beginnings of culture. Magic, religion, and science must be examined as active forces in human society, in organized cult and behavior, and in human psychology. In this we follow Frazer when he affirms that the simple truths derived from observation of nature have always been known to man. We also follow him when he tells us that "to live and to cause to live, to eat food, and beget children; these are the primary wants of man in the past, and they will be the primary wants of man in the future so long as the world lasts." Frazer tells us here in so many words that human culture is primarily founded on the biological needs of man.

Following this cue, we can add that in satisfying his primary biological needs through the instrumentalities of culture, man imposes new determinants on his behavior, that is, develops new needs. In the first place he must organize his tools, his artifacts, and his food-producing activities through the guidance of knowledge. Hence the need for primitive science, that is standardized, organized, and formulated principles of knowledge, must appear from the very beginnings of culture. Human action must be guided by the conviction of success. The stronger this conviction, the more effective the organization and execution of efforts. Hence magic, as the type of activity which satisfies this need of standardized optimism, is essential to the efficiency of human behavior. Finally, once man develops the need of building up systems of knowledge and anticipation, he is bound to inquire into the origins of humanity, into its destinies, and into the problems of life, death, and the universe. Hence, as a direct result of man's need to build systems and to organize knowledge, there emerges also the need for religion.

In all this we can see how a fuller insight into the nature of cultural phenomena, processes and instrumentalities leads us to reformulate evolutionary problems, yet without rejecting the principle of evolution, and the concepts of stages, survivals and origins. We begin also to see how such concepts can be defined. Thus the origins of science, religion and magic are not to be found in some single idea, corporate belief, or particular superstition; nor yet in a specific act of an individual or a group. By origins we mean the conditions, primeval and enduring, which determine the occurrence of a culturally established response, the conditions which, limited by scientific determinism, define the nature of an act, device, custom and institution. We mean the establishment of the primary biological need for such organized activities as the search for or production of food, the organization of mating and marriage, the building of houses, the production of clothing, and of primary tools and hunting weapons. When it comes to such aspects of culture as education, economics, law and government, we must be able to show how these forms of organization and types of activity are imposed upon primitive mankind by being indispensable to collective and concerted action.

The search for origins thus becomes really an analysis of cultural phenomena in relation, on the one hand, to man's biological endowment, and on the other, to his relationship to the environment. Since this type of general problem is solved by humanity in the development of a vast and increasingly complex instrumentality which we call culture, we are faced by another and now more frequently recognized problem: the question whether in the study of culture we can also discover general scientific laws of process, product, and interrelation. If culture, that is, the organized, implemented and purposeful behavior of man, carries its own determinism, then we can have a science of culture, we can establish general laws of culture, and without rejecting evolutionary or comparative studies in any way, we have to link them up with the scientific pursuit of understanding culture in general.

It will be well to illustrate this change in our scientific approach to the concept of origins by one or two more examples taken from Frazer's theory and from his handling and presentation of material. This is the more interesting in that the concept of origins has seldom been defined by such evolutionary students as Tylor, Morgan, McLennan, or Westermarck. Taking one theory of origins after another and comparing them, we would find an enormous diversity of theoretical implications, as well as of methods of establishment. The concept of origins usually means what occurred when the ape was struggling to become a man. To us the origins of marriage and promiscuity mean simply that the earliest man-ape had no regulations concerning his sexual conduct, and that complete anarchy reigned in all procreative relationships. When Westermarck affirms that marriage originated in a primeval form of monogamy, he tries to prove his case by showing that the highest anthropoid apes, as well as the lowest savages, live in single pairs. The origins of property in communism, the origins of religion in animism or totemism, usually amount to a more-or-less convincing proof that under primeval conditions man lived in social systems where communism or animism or the taboo reigned supreme. One of the favorite tricks of establishing origins consists in a more-or-less arbitrary assumption that this or that tribe or type of humanity is the standard primitive survival of earliest mankind. Whatever is found in such a tribe or group of tribes is assumed as most primitive. The central Australians, the Firelanders, the Veddas, the Bushmen have all been subject to this description as "lowest primitives." The Pygmy tribes scattered over Africa, Southeastern Asia, and the Indonesian Archipelago have been specially favored, because of their small stature and clear-cut distinctness from other tribes.

It is clear, however, that all such suggestions express rather the fertility of an ethnologist's imagination than any solid proof or argument. All surviving tribes whose arts and crafts correspond roughly to the paleolithic stage of pre-history are equally entitled to be candidates for primitiveness. Those aspects of their culture that can be related to its fundamental simplicity qualify as legitimate attributes of primitiveness. To take, however, one specific differential feature of this or that culture, and to affirm that it gives us the final clue to all riddles and origins, runs counter to the first principles of inductive reasoning.

Let us return to Frazer and to his views concerning the origins of marriage, the family and kinship. In *Totemism and Exogamy* this problem is fully treated, and the author accepts unreservedly the classical assumption that the origins of marriage are to be found in a complete sexual and parental promiscuity. This view is not held now by any anthropologist of repute. Frazer's attitude here is a genuine "survival." The real trouble with the assumption of primitive promiscuity lies in the faulty analysis of the institution of marriage which this hypothesis implies. As long as we think only of the sexual aspect of domesticity, there are no reasons why we could not assume that at the beginnings of culture there were no restrictions or only limited restrictions on "sexual communism." Marriage, however, is not just sexual intercourse, occasional or permanent. It is a contract between two people which implies the community of life under the same roof or shelter, cooperation in the household and in the management of property, but above all the production of legitimate children, whose care, education, and endowment for life is made obligatory on the parents. No one among the supporters of the hypothesis of promiscuity has ever tried to draw up even an imaginary picture of "communism in children." Such an attempt would have failed. No "survivals" of such communism can ever be found. Rivers has once or twice attempted to point out that we might perhaps be able to imagine communism in suckling of children. Such suggestions, however, are as unreal as they are merely imaginary and undocumented.

A careful and detailed scrutiny of the substance of the

matrimonial relationship, on a comparative basis, shows that the essence of marriage consists in the privilege of producing legitimate children, granted to bride and bridegroom by society in the contract of marriage. Under primitive conditions, and everywhere where a household constitutes an independent economic unit, this privilege has a great value. The duty of physiological tending, training, education and endowment of children is the counterpart of the privilege. We can thus state first that marriage as a legal contract is but a part and parcel of that wider and more fundamental institution, the family. And we can define marriage as the public, legal, and traditionally defined union by contract which gives the status of legitimacy to the children and an additional status to the married couple.

Here we can directly link up with the principle of Frazer quoted above. Man, primitive and civilized alike, needs the companionship of a mate; he also needs to reproduce. All these needs are integrated and implemented through the institution of marriage. This is a definition of marriage and the family; this also is the answer of what the origins of marriage and the family have been. From the very outset of culture the family has been the institution in which most of the fundamental needs of human beings have been satisfied. It is the institution primarily based on the reproductive need, but also directly associated with the production, distribution and consumption of food. It is the institution in which the continuity of culture, the handing over of tradition by the elder to the younger generation, is primarily carried out. Custom, order and authority are embodied in the family. The evolution of mankind, of its arts and crafts, of the various aspects of more complex institutions, can be studied with reference to such problems as to how kinship arose out of family ties, how clanship developed, and how individual households were integrated into the local group.

This brings us to one more interesting point in Frazer's theoretical treatment. Assuming, as he does, that sex was not regulated at the earliest stages of human development, he has to account for the advent of exogamy, that is of the strict and Draconic rules prohibiting the mating of kindred. Frazer, incidentally, does not make a clear-cut distinction between the prohibition of incest and the rules of exogamy. In this he follows Morgan's theory, which would place exogamy before incest as it places the clan before the family.

However this might be, Frazer develops here one of the least acceptable of his theories. Believing as he does that for a long time human beings paired and mated anyhow, and exactly as they liked, he has to assume an evolutionary phase, or moment at which something occurred which made them realize that it was better to prevent certain unions. To account for this he makes two assumptions. The first is that somehow or other the wise men of a primitive tribe came to the conclusion that incest and promiscuity were bad. Frazer discards the possibility that any really injurious effects of incest might have been assumed by primitives. He is even aware that biologically incest can hardly be proved to be damaging. Hence, something new had to be found. He therefore assumes that there existed a superstitious belief that incest was injurious to natural fertility. This belief then was translated into tribal law. "The scheme no doubt took shape in the minds of a few men of a sagacity and practical ability above the ordinary, who by their influence and authority persuaded their fellows to put it in practice." We have here, therefore, to assume that first there existed a state of primitive promiscuity; second, that an aversion to incest arose on superstitious grounds; third, that an extremely complicated system of social organization into moieties, clans, and marriage classes was devised so as to satisfy the superstitious fear; fourth, that this was implemented by an act of primitive legislators. It is hardly necessary to refute this theory in the light of our modern anthropological principles. We know that violent and revolutionary acts of legislation are characteristic of our present civilization, but do not occur in primitive humanity. We still would have to ask whether such a revolutionary legislative act occurred once and then spread by diffusion, or whether it occurred in many cases and always at the right moment.

Here also the full sociological analysis of marriage, parenthood, and kinship leads us to a much less spectacular, but very much simpler solution, founded on our understanding of human psychology and of the function of marriage and parenthood. Incest—and here we follow Freud without reservation—is a definite temptation within the family. Yet incest, if allowed to be practiced openly and lawfully, must become both psychologically and sociologically a disruptive force as regards the ties of family and marriage. On the psychological side incest would involve in the maturation of the young a complete reversal of all the sentiments between parent and child, as well as between brothers and sisters.

Sex, with its accompaniment of courtship, jealousies, and competitions, is not compatible with the attitude of reverence and submission characteristic of child-to-parent relations. It is not compatible with the protective, sober and coöperative relations between brothers and sisters. On the social side, sex with its intrinsic rivalries and jealousies would also induce chaos. Hence the elimination of the sexual motive from the family, and from its extended counterpart, the kinship group or the clan, is a fundamental need of social structure, primitive and civilized alike. Here, once more, we find the origins of a legal rule and of a fundamental aspect of the institution of marriage and family in the need which exists. The legal prohibition of incest and of mating between kindred is indispensable, because sexual relations are not compatible with intimate coöperative relations as between parents and children, brothers and sisters, and even near kinsmen and clansmen.

We could continue our analysis of the various details in Frazer's evolutionary treatment, which is perhaps most prominent in the fourth volume of his *Totemism and Exogamy*. Frazer propounds therein theories of the origins of shifting descent from female to male. He suggests the origins of agriculture from magic ceremonies intended to make seeds grow. He makes it plausible that the origins of art are to be found in certain magical practices.

In all such theories we find a strange divergence from the treatment of material contained in the constructive volumes, in which Frazer presents to us the well-integrated, well-contextualized picture of totemic systems, shot through occasionally by illuminating intuitive insight. The anthropologist knows well, also, Frazer's three theories of the origins of totemism. This material and the way in which he handles it prove clearly and conclusively that the origins of totemism must be read out of the nature and function of this belief, practice and institution. Totemism is a very concrete, simple and pragmatic way of establishing the relationship between man and nature. In its most developed forms, such as in central Australia and one or two parts of Africa, it is in reality a magical specialization in the control of primarily-important animal and plant species by man. Totemism in its pragmatically significant forms, that is, in the ritual management of natural fertility, is probably closely akin to magic. Frazer's second theory, seeking the origins of totemism in the rites of fertility and multiplication of the totem, is undoubtedly nearest to our present assessment of facts. For in this theory Frazer seeks for the origins of totemism in its most important function.

IV WHITHER ANTHROPOLOGY?

IN THIS CRITICAL ASSESSMENT of Frazer's work we find that in many ways he embodies a past epoch in anthropology and humanism, with many of its defects and with all its qualities. The material which he has given us, presented with such artistry of style and construction, will remain for long the standby of the ethnologist, and will be even of greater use to those who look for inspiration and collateral evidence in ethnographic materials. His single-minded devotion to scientific truth and to the understanding of humanity, primitive and civilized alike, makes his work essentially sound and true. It also makes it transcend very often, and transcend in the most fundamental points, many of his explicitly theoretical reflections.

The long road that starts in the woods of Nemi and leads us through primeval jungle, desert, swamp, South Sea Island, the steppes of Asia and the prairies of America, into a gradual understanding of the human heart and the human mind, is perhaps the greatest scientific Odyssey in modern humanism. We learn there at first hand to appreciate the behavior of primitive magicians, chiefs and kings. We become steeped in the live practices of savages at war and at work, in their marriage customs, the fears and hopes related to their taboos, to their tribal dances, and their military enterprises.

Frazer's theoretical position, his evolutionism, his comparative treatment of cultures, and his explanations by survival are at times not acceptable. Yet in the few passages here quoted—and they could be indefinitely multiplied—Frazer lays down the main principles of the modern scientific approach in anthropology. He believes in the essential similarity of the human mind and of human nature. He sees clearly that "human nature" has to be assessed primarily in terms of human needs; of those needs which permanently have to be answered if man is to survive, reproduce, live in order and security, and to progress. In his contextual treatment of the material he proves to us also that the primary necessities of mankind are satisfied through inventions, tools, weapons, and other material contrivances which, again, have to be managed by groups who coöperate and work and live in common, and where tradition is handed on from one generation to another. This implies that such characteristics of human groups as law, education, government, and economics are as necessary to man as his food, mating, and safety. His treatment of ethnological material, therefore, implies the theory of derived needs.

We have only to translate some of his somewhat simple evolutionary concepts into terms of the modern scientific analysis of culture in order to make them alive and real. Thus Frazer is as much the pioneer in modern scientific anthropology as the spokesman of his generation. The ground-work of his approach cannot be rejected. The comparative method is still the main theoretical tool for the formulation of general principles of anthropological science. The assumption of man's primary needs must remain the starting point in our inquiry into cultural phenomena. The evolutionary principle and its capital outfit will never become completely rejected by anthropology or humanism. Frazer's psychological interest appears to us sounder now than it seemed to be a quarter of a century ago.

Anthropology is even now divided by many schools, tendencies and partisan approaches. It is still in the fighting stage, engaged in the *bellum omnium contra omnes* so characteristic of early academic levels, if not of early humanity. This is perhaps the moment at which the squabbles, the skirmishes, and the fratricidal fights of anthropologists might be superseded gradually by an armistice, and the reign of constructive peace. We are beginning now to see clearly that evolutionism and the historical method, the principle of development and the fact of diffusion, explanations in terms of mental processes and sociological theories, are neither mutually exclusive nor intrinsically hostile, but complementary and inevitably correlated. This synthesis cannot be achieved in a little essay, but some general points can be here established.

The most comprehensive and most important movement, which also became a military campaign against evolutionism, started with the work of the German geographer and ethnologist, F. Ratzel. His positive contribution lies in the introduction of two concrete dimensions in the realm of the comparative study of races, tribes, and cultures. Fighting to overcome the "fear of time and fear of space" which he attributes to the evolutionist, he introduced the map of the world and the postulate of a more detailed chronology into all our speculations about origins and developments. Ratzel, with his keen geographic and historical sense, was able to see and to demonstrate that many parallels in artifact, device, custom and idea must be explained not on the principle that at a given stage of evolution certain similarities appear, but by the demonstration of direct contact between cultures and the spread of inventions through conveyance. Thus *diffusion,* as the taking-over of culture traits was termed, became the main principle of ethnographic explanation.

The school, developed above all in Germany, had its energetic sponsors in Great Britain, and there developed, under the influence of Franz Boas, a historical point of view among the anthropologists of the United States. What all such work had in common—the principles of a concrete treatment of each aspect of culture; the need of plotting out similarities or identities; the postulate that maps and time relations must always be kept in mind—was essentially sound and must be accepted into the outfit of all anthropological theory. Here it is necessary also to mention the addition made to anthropological theory by the ecologists and environmentalists. The most convincing and energetic spokesman of this point of view, Professor Ellsworth Huntington of Yale, has proved beyond doubt and cavil that the climate, and the natural resources of an environment, profoundly determine the history and the development of a culture which has been placed within that environment.

How can this concrete, historical, geographic and ecological approach be reconciled with evolutionism? The answer is simple. Contact between cultures, and the resulting transmission of arts and crafts, social forms, and ideas from one culture to another, are undeniably facts which have to be integrated into any theoretical approach, and which have to be incorporated into field-work and into all our hypotheses and principles. Frazer certainly held this point of view, and often explicitly used the concept of diffusion. Some evolutionists, however, have overlooked or neglected this factor, and in so far as this has occurred, their work has to be amended. On the other hand, the process of diffusion has been often very crudely and somewhat superficially defined by the diffusionists. Diffusion, that is, the conveyance of a cultural reality from one culture to another, is not an act, but a process closely akin in its working to any evolutionary process. For evolution deals above all with the influence of any type of "origins"; and origins do not differ fundamentally whether they occur by invention or by diffusion. Frazer himself assumes explicitly that the innovation which introduced the social ground-work for exogamy, and the rule of exogamy itself, originated within one tribe and then diffused to others. Clearly the new institution, whether invented or merely copied, produced the same historical, that is evolutionary, effects.

The problem, therefore, of whether a new trait occurs by invention or diffusion answers the concrete historical riddle in the space-time universe of discourse with reference to a given tribe at a given moment. The theory of how this new trait becomes incorporated into the culture, how it develops and through its development affects the culture as a whole, remains the same in both systems. The analysis into traits and trait-complexes, with which diffusionist schools have been working and are still working, will have to be amended and related to our general theory of what culture is, even more radically than is the case with evolutionary concepts. But the main principle that culture change must include the fact of contact and diffusion remains valid, and is the great contribution of Ratzel and his followers.

The need of a synthesis of anthropological methods, for a fuller understanding between the various partisan schools and mutually exclusive heresies, appears perhaps more directly today when anthropology, like every other discipline in social science, is called upon to play its part in actual present-day problems. Take the question of war. It has once more burst upon us, and we are faced with the vital question whether war as a type of human activity is part of man's doom, a heritage from his primeval ancestors, or an indispensable way of settling certain disputes. Here anthropology has a part to play. As the science of human beginnings and of human evolution, it can and it must answer the question whether war is primeval. This is not a matter of "origins," in the somewhat naïve sense of what occurred to the man-ape at the beginning of culture. It is rather the question whether war, like family, marriage, law and education, can be found in all human cultures at every stage of development, and more specifically whether it played an indispensable part at the earliest beginnings of mankind. For if it can be shown that war, that is, the collective settlement of intertribal problems by armed force, is not to be found at the beginnings of culture, this is a proof that war is not indispensable to the conduct of human affairs.

Most modern anthropologists would agree that war is neither primeval nor biologically founded—indeed, that it makes its appearance very late in human evolution, and that it subserves but a very limited range of needs, confined to one phase of evolution. Anthropology can also develop, through its comparative study of human institutions—political, such as the state or tribe-state; economic, such as slavery and serfdom; legal, such as the caste system and taxation—that most of the constructive and positive functions of war have been superseded by other agencies in our modern world, and that only its calamitous, destructive rôle persists. This rapid summary of my own views, elsewhere more fully documented,* might be taken as an example of the rôle which anthropology might play in clarifying some fundamental issues with which we are now faced.

Take the problems of government and the use of political force within a community as opposed to cultural organization. This is the problem of the state *versus* the nation. A full understanding of what we mean by nation-

* These views are elaborated in *Freedom and Civilization*, by Bronislaw Malinowski (New York, 1944). [Ed.]

ality as opposed to citizenship, which is the essence of nationalism as it has appeared during the last century and a half in human history, can also be supplied by a background of anthropological analysis. This would reveal that nationhood is a much older and more fundamental principle in evolution than the political organization of a police system, a tribe-state, or an empire. This would also show that the cultural autonomy of our modern nations would be enriched and revitalized by the limitation of political sovereignty, especially as regards the military self-determination of the state. I submit that for certain problems of post-war planning a full understanding of cultural integration as opposed to political control is essential, and that this can be provided by the comparative, evolutionary, and also historical contributions of anthropology.

Such concepts as democracy and freedom, communism and capitalism, the rôle of competition and of planning, can and must be submitted to a full anthropological analysis, inspired by the evolutionary as well as historical, psychological and sociological approaches. Problems of primitive law and order, of early forms of education and also of primitive types of science, magic, and religion, should be taken up with direct reference to the vital issues of today, and illuminated by the search for a common measure between the earlier and later forms studied, or by reaching out to questions of origins in terms of the fundamental rôle played by a type of activity, or by an institution in human development.

Anthropology can take up its serious rôle of *magistra vitae* side by side with history, in the classical sense of that word, and with other branches of humanism. The cross-fertilization of the social sciences is a concept which need not be pleaded for or developed here; it has been universally accepted. What, however, seems extremely important is the development of a more scientific basis for anthropology. This would in no way run counter to or undermine any of the "schools" or any of the component methods in the study of man. It would provide one and all of them with a firmer basis. Above all, diffusion, that is, culture change by contact, is a fact which anthropology has so far mainly projected into the earliest stages of human history, studies of which are inevitably reconstructive.

But at the present historical moment the phase and development through which we are now going is dominated by diffusion. The Western civilization, like a steam roller, is moving over the face of the world. The study of this cultural change, going on in Africa and Asia, in Oceania and in the New World, is the principal historical contribution of the ethnographer. Modern anthropology has already recognized this, and is becoming increasingly aware of its importance.

Culture change also is a practical problem which postwar reconstruction will have to face, and there is no doubt that after the present catastrophe is over the relations between races will have to be based on certain new principles of common rights, a share in privileges as well as duties, a coöperative collaboration and prosperity in which political, legal, and educational mechanisms will undergo a profound change. The anthropologist believes, on the one hand, in the right of all races, white, brown and black, and in the right of all minorities to equal treatment. He also has the conservative bias which makes him recognize the value of tradition, the value of the diversity of cultures, in their independence as well as in their cross-fertilization. His advice would be that our culture must not be imposed on others by the force of arms, the power of wealth, and the stringency of law.

The missionary spirit in the crudest form will have to be modified, at least. Nationalism, in the sense of a conservative reaction and the recognition of the integral value of its own culture by each nation, is spreading like wildfire all over the world. We, the members of the white race, are primarily responsible for that, and we have been giving our religion, our education, and many other spiritual boons to other races and other peoples, with an implied promise that once they accept our civilization they will become our equals. This promise has not been redeemed.

We are beginning now to see how dangerous it is to speak about the white man's burden, and to make others shoulder it and carry it for us. We give all the promises implied in our concept of human brotherhood and of equality through education, but when it comes to wealth, power, and self-determination we refuse this to other people.

Whether the anthropologist does not come too late into the picture, and whether his advice would still be of much value, even if he were allowed to take part at any conference table of the high and mighty, is one question. That the anthropologist cannot remain silent is another. His advice would be to give the maximum of self-determination to every cultural group, or even minority. He has always believed in Indirect Rule, as this has recently been introduced in the British colonies. Indirect rule means self-government by any tribe or nation in cultural matters, under the advisory control of the ruling power. Here comes another important point. In the future reconstruction of the world, the most important principles must be determined by our crying need of collective security. This means concretely that large political units must not be allowed to maintain their armaments, military apparatus and economic autarchy, especially if there is no control whatever over their military aggressive tendencies. What we need in the future is less political independence for powerful states, and no increased political —which is ultimately military—self-determination for groups and units who have no military sovereignty in their hands as yet. Hence, the anthropologist would not preach the creation of numerous small tribal states in Africa, each completely independent politically, that is, encouraged to wage war against its neighbors. The anthropologist would not preach the building of large armies in China or India without some form of international control; for without it, all the dangers of the present conditions of the balance of power would increase. It would not in any way contribute towards the cultural independence of these great or small nations. As a scientific moralist fully in sympathy with races hereto oppressed or at least underprivileged, the anthropologist would demand equal treatment for all, full cultural independence for every differential group or nation, no political sovereignty for any tribe, state, kingdom, republic, or empire.

All this may be Utopian and visionary. It is, however, fundamentally sound from the point of view of the scientific analysis of culture as a whole. Above all, the better we come to understand, and the more fully we study and reflect upon the relation between culture and political power, the more clearly we come to the conclusion that force must be dissociated from partisan or from differential interests, and placed in the hands of a disinterested controlling agency. Culture as a way of life, as a national type of pursuit, taste and interest, cannot be dictated, controlled or legislated. It ought to be given the best conditions for development, and cross-fertilization with outside influences, but left to maintain its own balance and its own development under conditions of full autonomy.

In all this we may seem to have wandered far away from our culture-hero, Frazer, and from his work. This is not so. Frazer was a great humanist. In his work and his approach there was the mellow blend of conservative love for tradition, for the differential elements in each culture and every stage of development, with a keen sense for the need of progress, reason, and equity. He was able to appreciate the strangest, the most exotic, and most savage qualities, and to read into them their essentially human meaning. He was also able to read out of them, as in *Psyche's Task*, the germs of creative influences and of future development. His humanistic philosophy was to live and to let live. His monumental works, which give us a picture of primitive humanity and its contemporary counterparts, provide a background against which we can reformulate the new scientific type of anthropology, and learn to appreciate that the study of human thought, belief, and action must be inspired not merely by the artistic touch of literary genius, but above all, by full human sympathy extending even to the humblest, simplest, and most defenceless manifestations of mankind.

INDEX

Activities, and rules, 53; classified, 110; need for, 106
African culture, research in, 80
Age-groups, function of, 116
Agricultural ritual, 190
Ancient Society, 24
Animal behavior, and culture, 133
Animism, 19; Tylor on, 26-27
Ankermann, B., 20, 32
Anthropology, and nationalism, 219; and war, 215ff; behaviorism and, 23, 71; comparative method, 18; concepts and methods, 15ff; conflict of schools, 212ff; Frazer's position in, 187ff; functional axioms, 150; functionalism in, 18, 147ff; historical method, 15, 19ff; institutions in, 39ff; practical rôle of, 215ff; psychoanalysis and, 22; psychological method, 19, 31; scope of, 3ff, 11ff; sociological viewpoint, 19; sources of, 3, 15; survivals, 28ff, 142, 202, 205; trait diffusion, 31ff
"Anthropology," article on, 31
Archaeology, and anthropology, 21
Art, function of, 174
Artifacts, as culture elements, 20; invention of, 134-135; rôle in culture, 151
Associations, function of, 55ff, 116
Authority, 129ff; in social groups, 61
Axioms, of functionalism, 150; of needs, 171

Bachofen, J., 26, 176, 194
Bandelier, A. F., 21
Bastian, Adolf, 4
Bechterev, V., 133

Behaviorism, 23, 71
Bemba, v
Bergson, H., 184
Biological basis of culture, 36, 75ff, 109; determinism, 121
Boas, Franz, 32, 214
Bodily comforts, and culture, 91ff
Bougainville, L. A. de, 15
Bouglé, C. C., 183
Bride-price, 30
Briffault, Robert, 26, 176
Bücher, K., 148

Cambridge Expedition, 183
Capital, concept of, 127
Causes, search for, 117-118
Chagga, v
Change, cultural, 41, 215, 218
Charlevoix, P. S. X. de, 148
Charter, 140, 162; and function, 111; of groups, 48ff, 52; of tribe-state, 165
Children of the Sun, 25
Clan, function of, 168ff
Clans, totemic, 57-58
Classificatory kinship, 25, 29, 156
Climate, Huntington on, 214
Consciousness, 23, 138
Conservatism, in culture, 218
Contiguity, as cultural factor, 56-57
Contrat social, 43
Commissariat, 97ff, 113, 155, 172
Comparative method, 18; Frazer and, 212
Complex, and trait, 31ff, 33, 215
Copernicus, 11
Crawley, E., 19, 26, 183
Cultural determinism; *see* Determinism, cultural
Culture, analysis of, 150; and ani-